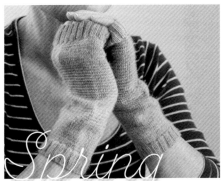

A YEAR OF
TECHNIQUES

Twelve projects to upgrade your knitting skills

ARNALL-CULLIFORD KNITWEAR

Foreword

KAY GARDINER & ANN SHAYNE

Remember the day you learned to knit?

It was so unfamiliar – we do recall that. The oddness of the motions, the yarn that had a mind of its own, the indecipherable code of a pattern. Whose hands are those attached to our arms? They are not behaving!

Maybe you learned to knit from a friend, your mom, your grandmother. Maybe you took a class. Or watched a video online. However you learned to knit, it happened: you turned yarn into fabric.

Which is a small way to describe an instant, white-hot obsession. If you're like the knitters we know, your vocabulary suddenly shifted.

> "Just one more row."
> "Sshhhh, I'm *counting*."
> "I have to go run an errand" – code, of course, for "I'm going to the yarn shop. Again."

Suddenly, an endless, delightful puzzle presented itself, and the more we knitted, the more we discovered that there's more to discover.

In the months that we have been making the projects in *A Year of Techniques*, we have had this feeling over and over again – the pure delight of learning something new. We have been knitting for decades, and sometimes we get pretty full of ourselves about the clever things we can make. But Jen and Jim Arnall-Culliford show us in *A Year of Techniques* that there is always something new to learn – and this programme of projects and lessons is unlike anything we've ever seen.

The idea of tying each month's technique to a new project means that we are never stuck with a pile of swatches. Instead, we're stockpiling holiday gifts with absolutely no stress.

The designs are clever, achievable in a short time, and represent a who's who of designers. When we first saw the list of participants, we knew *A Year of Techniques* was going to be something extraordinary: Ella Austin, Martina Behm, Rachel Coopey, Ella Gordon, Sarah Hatton, Rosemary (Romi) Hill, Bristol Ivy, Mary Jane Mucklestone, Tin Can Knits, Woolly Wormhead. These are all designers working at the peak of the game. Their inventive minds bring us design after design with twists and surprises.

At the head of the class, of course, fearlessly leading the way, are Jen and Jim Arnall-Culliford. Teaching knitting is a rare skill, and Jen is a walking, talking encyclopaedia of knowledge about the most arcane aspects of virtually any technique. Even more amazing, she is completely unflappable and cool headed about it all – her tutorial videos convey a calm and confidence that leave us nodding along with her, "Sure, no big deal. Piece of cake." Even when we're wondering if we can actually figure it out.

Which, thanks to her careful explanations, we can.

We're climbing Mount Intarsia. We're making stripes that chase each other around but never catch each other. We're making mice. We're learning something new every month, and as each project begins, we have the exact same feeling that we had on that day we learned to knit.

This. Is. So. Fun.

Introduction

JIM ARNALL-CULLIFORD

"Wouldn't it be great if…" conversations all too often end up being dreams that never materialise. Sometimes, however, these vague ideas crystallise into something that actually comes together. *A Year of Techniques* started as just such a conversation. Over our company Christmas party – a quiet lunch on a dreary, grey January day – we were tossing around ideas for a new project. Obviously, it was going to be a book of some sort about knitting, but how could we put our stamp on it to make it stand out?

One of the joys of working on patterns for lots of designers is that you get to pick up on the myriad of different ways that they achieve similar ends. The challenge of coming to terms with an unusual technique is what keeps us going. A book for teaching useful and interesting techniques, would draw on our experiences not only as technical editors, but also on our time as school teachers. An instructional manual would be tricky to make anything other than dry, so we knew that we would want designs to match each of the skills. While we both have published designs and have contributed designs to *A Year of Techniques,* we wanted to bring in experts in each area to give us their take on a particular method. We then had to think about a theme for the book and the number of techniques and patterns that should be in it. I initially suggested patterns by season, but once we'd agreed on 12 patterns, it was hardly a great leap to have a month-by-month model.

Knitting and learning are both activities that can be done alone, but are often more enjoyable and effective in company. We wanted to include some collaborative, community aspect to the project, in addition to working with our band of talented designers. This is difficult to achieve with a printed book if the readers are scattered all over the world. The solution of course was to get content and discussions online so anyone could get involved. We have been lucky to have been able to work with the outstanding Jesse Wild in shooting videos so that Jen can walk you through how to do something, and explain why you might want to in the first place, from the comfort of your own home. Furthermore, the knitalong threads on both the Arnall-Culliford Knitwear group on Ravelry and in The Lounge on Mason-Dixon Knitting have so far proven to be fertile ground for sharing tips, problems and above all enjoyment of knitting something new.

You can use this book in a number of ways. Should you wish to learn a particular technique, we have produced the tutorials to be as generic as possible, backed up by the video tutorials hosted at Mason-Dixon Knitting, so you can apply the technique to any pattern. On the other hand, you can simply dip in and out of the patterns, using the tutorials as you need them. You could of course work through the whole year and, if you do, you'll find that while some months stand alone with their technique, others use techniques encountered in preceding months.

As someone, somewhere has said many times, it doesn't matter whether you've been knitting for five minutes, five years, or five decades – **there's always something new to learn.** So here it is: a book of 12 lessons to take you beyond the basics of knitting, backed up by irresistible projects and a thriving online community to travel with you through your year of techniques.

Jen and Jim Arnall-Culliford

Tutorials

Contents

Spring

March

TECHNIQUE **Helical Stripes**
PROJECT **Hyacinthus Armwarmers**
DESIGNER **Jen Arnall-Culliford**

April

TECHNIQUE **Intarsia**
PROJECT **Brambling Shawl**
DESIGNER **Bristol Ivy**

May

TECHNIQUE **Pinhole Cast On**
PROJECT **Alex the Mouse**
DESIGNER **Ella Austin**

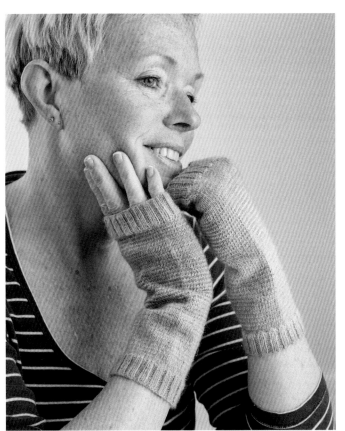
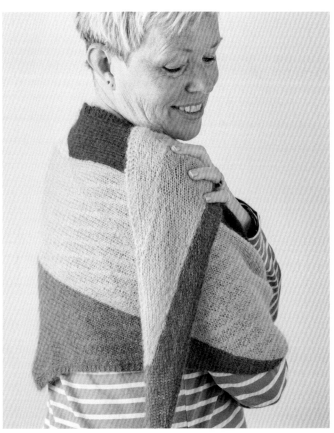

TECHNIQUE
HELICAL STRIPES

To get us warmed up and in the zone for tackling new skills in our knitting, we will start with one of my favourite knitting tricks. This technique is so simple and yet so clever, that when I first came across it, I couldn't help but cast on for what became my first published knitting pattern.

Many knitting projects are best worked in the round, since the finished item will be based on a tube – hats, mittens and sleeves are all good examples, as they would otherwise require seaming. When stripes are worked in the round, there is an inevitable "jog" at the start of the round, where the end of the previous round in one colour sits next to the start of the round in a new colour. There are various possibilities for minimising this step in the colour changes, but only helical stripes completely eliminate the jog. Sadly, the helical method can only create stripes of limited width (up to a 4-row stripe repeat is possible, but beyond that it becomes tricky to manage), but for single row stripes they are magical.

TRADITIONAL STRIPES

In traditional single row stripes, the yarn not in use is dropped at the end of each round, and then carried up to the next round where it is required. This creates a jog in the stripes at the start of the round (1), and a ridge on the wrong side, where the yarns are carried (2). In helical stripes, the rounds sit on top of one another as helices, so there is no jog and no yarn carrying required.

HELICAL STRIPES

The basic method for helical stripes is that you work two (or more) continuous spirals of stitches, sitting on top of each other. I like to imagine it as the yarns chasing each other around, but never quite catching up! While working helical stripes, you are working less than a round each time, so where you finish knitting on each "round" will change. The start of the round marker remains in the fabric to enable you to place design elements later (such as a thumb or heel). It is possible to work entire rounds in both yarns, but this makes it much trickier to maintain even tension at the end of the round. Therefore the small inconvenience of slipping a few stitches each round is definitely worth the effort.

HELICAL GARTER STITCH

Like stripe patterns worked in the round, garter stitch in the round also creates a jog, where a knit stitch from the previous round sits next to a purl stitch in the new round (and vice versa). For a jogless garter stitch in the round, work helical stripes with two balls of the same colour yarn, and use one ball to knit and the other to purl.

STEPWISE INSTRUCTIONS FOR HELICAL STRIPES

In the following instructions yarn A is the blue yarn and yarn B is the yellow yarn.

i   Work at least 1 round in yarn A.
ii Join in yarn B (leaving yarn A attached).

iii With yarn B, knit to 3 sts before end of round.

iv Slip 3 sts purlwise from left to right needle, to reach the end of the round.

v   Pick up yarn A ready to work the next stitch.

vi With yarn A, knit until there are 3 sts in yarn B remaining on left needle.

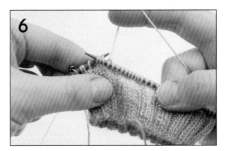

vii Slip 3 sts purlwise from left to right needle, to reach yarn B.

viii Pick up yarn B and knit until there are 3 sts in yarn A remaining on left needle.
ix   Slip 3 sts purlwise from left to right needle, to reach yarn A.

Working steps vi–ix creates helical stripes.

WHAT TO DO IF YOU "CATCH UP"
Particularly when working shaping at the same time as helical stripes, just take care never to work over the last stitch in the previous colour. If, for example, yarn A does "catch up" with yarn B whilst you are in the middle of working your thumb shaping, you will need to work as follows:
Unknit as many stitches as you need to, so that you have 3 sts in yarn B remaining on the left needle. Slip those 3 stitches purlwise to the right needle so that you reach yarn B. Knit around in yarn B until there are 3 sts remaining in yarn A. Slip 3 sts purlwise, and continue where you left off with yarn A, not forgetting to complete any shaping.

USING DOUBLE-POINTED NEEDLES

The instructions on page 11 (and those in the Hyacinthus Armwarmer pattern) can be used for working helical stripes with any kind of needle. However, when working with double-pointed needles (dpns), the method can be slightly altered to make for an even easier process where there is no need to slip any stitches. This method uses the fact that you can leave yarn accessible at the end of any of the needles. You can then choose to return to that yarn at any time, without needing to slip stitches to reach it.

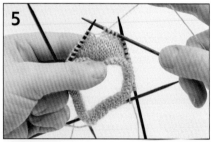

v Return to yarn A, and knit 2 needles' worth of stitches (2 and 3).

Repeat steps v and vi as required. You will notice that you stop working with one colour when you reach the needle just completed by the last colour. The yarns never catch up with each other, and at no point is either yarn carried up the inside of the work.

STEPWISE INSTRUCTIONS FOR WORKING WITH DPNS

In the following instructions yarn A is the pale green yarn and yarn B is the yellow yarn.

i   Work at least 1 round in yarn A.
ii Distribute your stitches roughly evenly over 4 needles (use a 5th needle to knit onto).
iii Join in yarn B.

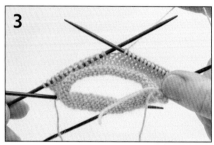

vi Pick up yarn B. Then knit 2 needles' worth of stitches (4 and 5).

OTHER APPLICATIONS OF HELICAL STRIPES

Helical stripes have a number of applications beyond just working jogless one-row stripes. When knitting with hand-dyed yarn you are often advised to work stripes from two skeins in order to disguise any differences in dyeing between the skeins. If you are working your garment in the round, traditional stripes would require carrying the yarn at the change of round marker, whereas helical stripes are essentially invisible, making them ideal for this application. I use a section of helical stripes to blend from one skein to the next – starting a helical section when I have about 15% of the skein remaining.

VARIATIONS ON A THEME

Want to work with more colours? That's absolutely fine! Divide your round into roughly equal sections (you can use stitch markers or dpns) – the same number of sections as the number of colours you want to use. Work the first round by knitting each section with a

iv With yarn B, knit 3 needles' worth of stitches. You can see that yarn B is located at the bottom right hand corner, and yarn A is located at the bottom left hand corner.

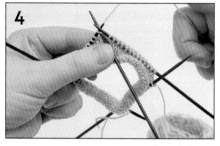

new colour of yarn. Subsequent stripes are then worked by *knitting until you have 3 stitches remaining on your left needle before the next colour change. Slip those 3 stitches to the right needle, and pick up the next colour. Repeat from * as required.

Slipped stitch patterns work really well with helical stripes. Keep one ball of yarn working just knit stitches, and then try slipping stitches at regular intervals with the other yarn. For example, with a pattern using 72 stitches per round, if you slip every 4th stitch with one yarn you will end up with vertical stripes. You can vary this further by choosing a number that isn't a multiple of your stitch count. For example, if you slip the 5th stitch each time, and have 71 sts in your round, you will make a spiral pattern of slipped stitches.

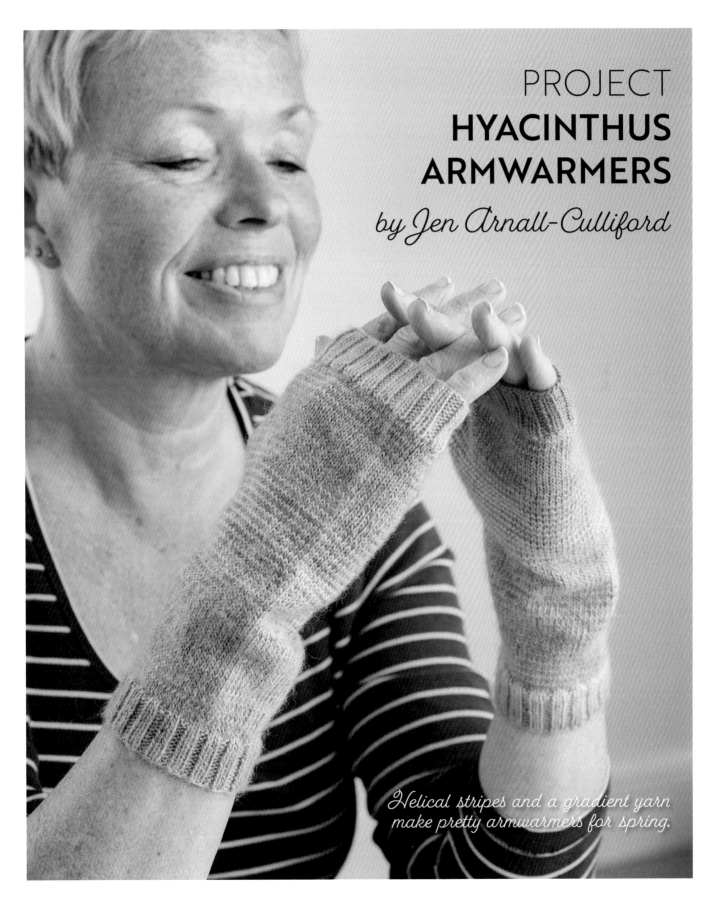

PROJECT
HYACINTHUS ARMWARMERS
by Jen Arnall-Culliford

Helical stripes and a gradient yarn make pretty armwarmers for spring.

March

SIZE
To fit average adult
Armwarmer circumference: 19cm [7½in]
Length: 21.5cm [8½in]

YARN
Schoppel Wolle Zauberball (4ply weight; 75% wool, 25% nylon; 420m per 100g ball)
Snickelway / Bunte Gasse (2310); 1 x 100g ball (the yarn will be wound into two balls, named yarns A and B)

NEEDLES AND NOTIONS
1 set 2.5mm [US 1½] needles of your preferred type for working small circumferences in the round, or size needed to match tension
Stitch markers
Waste yarn

TENSION
38 sts and 50 rounds to 10cm [4in] over helical stripe pattern, after washing and blocking

ABBREVIATIONS
A full list of abbreviations appears on the inside back cover.

PATTERN NOTES
The single row stripes created by the helical stripe method look best when there is good contrast between the colours of the two balls of yarn you create. If you find the colour at the start of the second ball is very close to the colour of the first ball, it is well worth winding some yarn off the second ball before joining it in to ensure a good contrast. In the same way, when you come to make your second armwarmer, you may choose to wind off some yarn so that it starts with a similar colour to your first armwarmer. The colour repeats in a Zauberball don't always match each other exactly, so making identical armwarmers would be a challenge, but using a similar colour for the ribbing helps to create a visual sense of matching.

ARMWARMER

MAKE 2 ALIKE
Please take the time to read carefully through the tutorial on helical stripes (page 10).
Wind your yarn into two equal balls. If you are using a Zauberball it is better to do this by hand, rather than using a ball winder, to avoid tangles. Decide which ball is to be yarn A, and which is yarn B.

1 ARM CUFF
With yarn A, cast on 72 sts. Distribute your sts over your needles, taking care not to twist, pm and join for working in the round.
Round 1: *K2, p2; repeat from * to end.
Last round sets 2x2 rib. Work a further 11 rounds in 2x2 rib as set.
Knit 1 round.

2 ARM
Now work in helical stripes as follows (see photo tutorial for further assistance):
Join in yarn B (leaving yarn A attached).
With yarn B, knit to 3 sts before end of round.
Slip 3 sts purlwise from the left to the right needle to reach the end of the round.
*With yarn A, knit until there are 3 sts in yarn B remaining on left needle.
Slip 3 sts purlwise from left to right needle, to reach yarn B.
With yarn B, knit until there are 3 sts in yarn A remaining on left needle.
Slip 3 sts purlwise from left to right needle, to reach yarn A.*
Working from * to * creates helical stripes.

Continue to work in helical stripes until armwarmer measures 13cm [5in] from cast-on edge.

3 THUMB GUSSET
Continue to work in helical stripes as described above, and AT THE SAME TIME, you will shape the thumb gusset as follows:

All thumb gusset shaping is worked in yarn A (yarn B is always just knitted, slipping the markers as you reach them).
While you are using yarn A, work the increases as you reach the start of round marker as follows:
Slm, kfb, k1, kfb, pm. *2 sts inc; 74 sts.*

Work thumb inc as follows when you next reach the start of round marker and are using yarn A (looking at your knitted fabric there will be one knitted yarn B round above your first yarn A thumb inc):
Slm, kfb, knit to last st before marker, kfb, slm. *2 sts inc.*

Note:
You may find that you need to switch yarns to work your stripes in the middle of your thumb shaping. This is fine, just don't forget to complete the shaping when you return to yarn A.

Continue to work helical stripes and repeat thumb increases each time yarn A reaches the start of the round marker, until you have 23 thumb sts between the markers (a total of 10 increase rounds have been worked). *92 sts.*

Work in helical stripes until the next time yarn A reaches the start of round marker, then separate the thumb sts as follows (if your colour change is in the middle of the gusset, see note below):
Slm, k1, sl next 22 sts to waste yarn. Cast on 2 sts using the backwards loop method. Remove thumb gusset marker. *72 sts.*

Note:
If your yarn B is in the middle of your thumb gusset when you come to separate for your thumb: Slip stitches so that you are at yarn B. Knit on in yarn B until you are safely off the thumb gusset (you can knit right round to just before the start of the round again, or just a bit – it's up to you). Then slip back to yarn A and separate the thumb as per the instructions.

4 HAND
Now continue to work helical stripes with no further shaping until armwarmer measures 19cm [7½in] from cast-on edge.

Work in helical stripes until yarn B reaches the end of round marker and break yarn. Move sts around your needles so that you return to the last st worked in yarn A, which should be on your right needle. Knit with yarn A to end of round marker.

5 CUFF
With yarn A, work 12 rounds in 2x2 rib as set at arm cuff (step 1). Cast off all sts, using a larger needle if necessary so that the edge isn't too tight.

6 THUMB
Return 22 thumb sts to needles. With yarn A, pick up and knit 4 sts along the cast-on edge at the base of the thumb. Pm for start of round.
Round 1: Knit to last 4 sts, ssk, k2tog. *2 sts dec; 24 sts.*
Round 2: *K2, p2; repeat from * to end.
Last round sets 2x2 rib. Work a further 11 rounds in 2x2 rib.
Cast off all sts, using a larger needle if necessary so that the edge isn't too tight.

7 FINISHING
Weave in all ends but do not trim.
Soak your armwarmers in lukewarm water and wool wash for 20 minutes. Squeeze out excess water (but do not wring). Press between towels to dry further. Lay your armwarmers flat to dry, paying attention to fold them neatly along the thumb. When they are completely dry, trim any remaining ends.

TECHNIQUE
INTARSIA

Now that we are nicely warmed up after working some helical stripes, it's time to take on a technique that many knitters find a bit intimidating: intarsia.

There are many ways of incorporating multiple colours into your knitting. From the simplest stripes, to slipped stitch, stranded (or Fair Isle) and intarsia designs, the arrangement of colours within your knitting will determine which method is required. For designs with just one colour per row, then stripes or slipped stitch patterns will be used. But when you work with more than one colour in each row or round of knitting, you will be using either the stranded or intarsia methods.

For stranded knitting, you use all the colours (generally just two, but sometimes more) right the way across the row or round. As the colours are used throughout, they are carried on the wrong side of the work when not in use. Intarsia is required when the colours are used in blocks, and each block of colour needs its own ball of yarn. When changing from one colour to the next you need to twist your yarns together to join the two blocks of colour, and avoid holes. This tutorial will explain how to work that twist, as well as showing you a neat way to weave in your ends.

As a new knitter I dived in to projects, always aiming to learn something new. Over the months I ticked off many skills – cables, lace, socks, Fair Isle – and nothing slowed me down, until I tried an intarsia project. As an experienced knitter I now know that the project I chose was completely unrealistic, but at the time it was enough to convince me that intarsia and I would never be friends. Over the years I've discovered that I'm not alone in this early experience of intarsia, and many very seasoned knitters still have a strong aversion to this handy colourwork technique.

This month's beautiful Brambling Shawl by Bristol Ivy will show you that intarsia doesn't need to be frustrating. Bristol combines intarsia colour blocks with shaping, so that you are always working stitches in the same shade on each row. If a stitch was worked in dark grey on the previous row, it will be worked in dark grey in the next row (with the exception of when new colours are introduced). More complicated intarsia designs require you to think ahead and plan where you will next use a colour, and thus yarns may need to be carried from one colour change to another. Here, there is no need to carry your yarns along the rear of the work, so massively decreasing the complexity of this project. Brambling also uses a maximum of 4 colours of yarn in a row, which keeps the tangling of balls to a manageable level. Indeed, this shawl is a surprisingly portable project, making it perfect for commuter knitting or knit night with friends.

STEPWISE INSTRUCTIONS FOR TWISTING YOUR YARNS (IT)

i Start the row by ensuring that your yarns are not tangled.

ii Work in pattern until you reach the colour change. In this pattern the y-markers denote the change from one colour to the next.

iii Slip the marker, then hold the old yarn over the new yarn before working the first stitch in the new colour.

iv Give the first stitch in the new colour a little tug to ensure that the tension is even.

v Work in pattern to the next colour change. Then repeat the same process. Slip the y-marker then hold the old yarn over the new yarn as you work the first stitch in the new colour.

vi Give the first stitch in the new colour a tug to ensure that it is tight enough.

vii At the end of the row, you will see that your working yarns are twisted with each other.

Untwist them before starting the next row.

viii The process on wrong side rows is exactly the same. Work in pattern to the colour change. Slip the y-marker then hold the old yarn over the new yarn before working the first stitch in the new yarn.

ix Give the first stitch in the new colour a tug to keep the tension even.

x Continue in this way, untangling your yarns again at the end of the row.

STEPWISE INSTRUCTIONS FOR WEAVING IN ENDS

Having joined in a new colour and worked a few rows, it can be really helpful to weave in your ends. Doing so will tidy up the area where you worked the first stitch.

i Thread the tail of your yarn onto a tapestry needle.

ii On the wrong side of the work, sew the yarn along the twisted join between the two colours, working up and down through the loops formed by the intarsia twists.

iii Give the fabric a good stretch in each direction to ensure that the yarn isn't puckering the fabric.

iv Leave the ends untrimmed until after you have blocked your finished shawl. This helps to avoid the trimmed end poking through to the right side of the fabric.

BUILDING ON YOUR INTARSIA SKILLS

Having mastered the vertical intarsia twist that's used in the Brambling Shawl, you may wish to expand your intarsia skills to more complex designs. There are various factors that will determine how tricky a particular design is. These might include the following:

❖ The type of yarn used – stretchier yarns will be more forgiving of any tension issues where the colours join, whereas slippery yarns will make it much harder to keep ends and joins tidy.
❖ The number of different colours used in each row – more colours means more joins, and thus each join needs to be neater to give the same overall impression.
❖ How regular the shapes are – straight vertical and horizontal joins are easiest, followed by diagonals that shift by 1 stitch each time; irregular shapes will require most yarn management and planning of where to leave ends.

Geometric designs with fewer colours, knitted in wool, would be a good next step, whereas a complex picture knit with many colours might be a bit more challenging. Not that there's anything wrong with choosing a challenging project, as long as you know what you're taking on!

When working a design with regular motifs, like the classic tumbling blocks pattern popularised by Kaffe Fassett, it is really helpful to work out how much yarn is required for each block of colour. You can then wind off the precise amount needed, and either leave the yarn dangling loose, or wind it onto bobbins as required. The benefit of leaving the yarns hanging loose is that you can just pull them out of any tangle created by the intarsia twists.

PROJECT
BRAMBLING
SHAWL
by Bristol Ivy

Intersecting curves are created using a clever combination of intarsia and shaping.

April

SIZE
Wingspan: 216cm [85in]
Depth at centre: 41.5cm [16¼in]

YARN
Fyberspates Cumulus (4ply weight; 74% baby Suri alpaca, 26% Mulberry silk; 150m per 25g ball)
Yarn A: Slate; 1 x 25g ball
Yarn B: Camel; 1 x 25g ball
Yarn C: Silver; 1 x 25g ball
Yarn D: Plum; 1 x 25g ball
Yarn E: Sea Green; 1 x 25g ball

NEEDLES AND NOTIONS
1 pair or 1 set 4mm [US 6] straight or circular needles, or size needed to match tension
2 different types of stitch marker (x and y)

TENSION
20 sts and 28 rows to 10cm [4in] over st st, after washing and blocking

ABBREVIATIONS
IT(y) intarsia twist (and slip y-marker); hold the old yarn over the new yarn ready to work the next stitch (and then slip y-marker); see photo tutorial for further assistance

A full list of abbreviations appears on the inside back cover.

STITCHES INCREASED AND DECREASED
Each time a total stitch count is given, it is also stated how many sts have been increased or decreased since the last total stitch count. Where sections are repeated, the total stitch counts are not given, but rather the change in sts is indicated where relevant.

SHAWL

1 WORK INCREASES
With yarn A, cast on 7 sts.
Set-up row (WS): K3, pmx, k1, pmx, k3.
Row 1 (inc, RS): K3, slmx, M1R, knit to end. *1 st inc.*
Row 2 (WS): K3, slmx, purl to x-marker, slmx, k3.
Row 3: Knit.
Row 4: Rep row 2.
These 4 rows set the garter stitch edging (indicated by the x-markers) and the shawl body increase pattern (1 st inc every 4 rows).

Rows 5–36: Rep rows 1–4 a further 8 times. *9 sts inc; 16 sts.*

2 WORK INCREASES, INTRODUCE YARN B
Row 37 (inc, RS): K3, slmx, M1R, knit to 3 sts before x-marker, k2tog, pmy, join in yarn B and with yarn B, k1, M1R, slmx, k3. *1 st inc; 17 sts.*

Now that yarn B has been joined in, it will shift on every 3rd row, increasing the number of yarn B stitches and decreasing the number of yarn A stitches. The shawl body increases continue to occur on every 4th row.

Row 38 (WS): With yarn B, k3, slmx, purl to y-marker, ITy, with yarn A, purl to x-marker, slmx, k3.
Row 39: With yarn A, knit to y-marker, ITy, with yarn B, knit to end.
Row 40 (shift B, WS): With yarn B, k3, slmx, purl to 1 st before y-marker, M1P-R, p1, ITy, with yarn A, p2tog, purl to x-marker, slmx, k3.
Row 41 (inc): With yarn A, k3, slmx, M1R, knit to y-marker, ITy, with yarn B, knit to end. *1 st inc.*
Row 42: With yarn B, k3, slmx, purl to y-marker, ITy, with yarn A, purl to x-marker, slmx, k3.
Row 43 (shift B, RS): With yarn A, knit to 2 sts before y-marker, k2tog, ITy, with yarn B, k1, M1R, knit to end.
Row 44: Rep row 42.
Row 45 (inc): With yarn A, k3, slmx, M1R, knit to y-marker, ITy, with yarn B, knit to end. *1 st inc.*

Row 46: Rep shift B WS (row 40).
Row 47: Rep row 39.
Row 48: Rep row 42.
Row 49 (inc, shift B, RS): With yarn A, k3, slmx, M1R, knit to 2 sts before y-marker, k2tog, ITy, with yarn B, k1, M1R, knit to end. *1 st inc.*
Row 50: Rep row 42.

Rows 51–74: Rep rows 39–50 twice more. *9 sts inc; 26 sts total (9 sts in yarn A and 17 sts in yarn B).*

3 WORK INCREASES, INTRODUCE YARN C
Row 75 (RS): Work in yarn A as set to y-marker, ITy, with yarn B, knit to 3 sts before x-marker, k2tog, pmy, join yarn C and with yarn C, k1, M1R, slmx, k3.

Now that yarn C has been joined in, it will shift on every 4th row (the RS rows where you are NOT working shawl body incs), increasing the number of yarn C stitches. Yarn B will continue to shift on every 3rd row, thus increasing the number of yarn B stitches and decreasing the number of yarn A stitches. The shawl body increases continue to occur on every 4th row.

Row 76 (WS): With yarn C, k3, slmx, purl to y-marker, ITy, with yarn B, purl to y-marker, ITy, with yarn A, purl to x-marker, slmx, k3.
Row 77 (inc, shift B, RS): With yarn A, k3, slmx, M1R, knit to 2 sts before y-marker, k2tog, ITy, with yarn B, k1, M1R, knit to y-marker, ITy, with yarn C, knit to end. *1 st inc; 27 sts.*
Row 78: Rep row 76.
Row 79 (shift C, RS): Work in yarn A as set to y-marker, ITy, with yarn B, knit to 2 sts before y-marker, k2tog, ITy, with yarn C, k1, M1R, knit to end.
Row 80 (shift B, WS): With yarn C, k3, slmx, purl to y-marker, ITy, with yarn B, purl to 1 st before y-marker, M1P-R, p1, ITy, with yarn A, p2tog, purl to x-marker, slmx, k3.
Row 81 (inc): With yarn A, k3, slmx, M1R, knit to y-marker, ITy, with yarn B, knit to y-marker, ITy, with yarn C, knit to end. *1 st inc; 28 sts.*
Row 82: Rep row 76.

SCHEMATIC

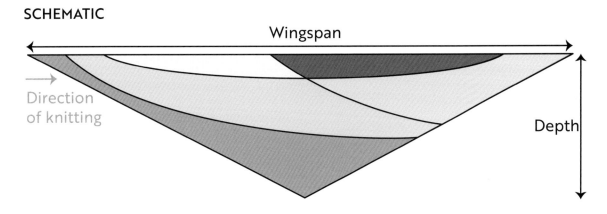

Row 83 (shift B and C, RS): Work in yarn A as set to 2 sts before y-marker, k2tog, ITy, with yarn B, k1, M1R, knit to 2 sts before y-marker, k2tog, ITy, with yarn C, k1, M1R, knit to end.
Row 84: Rep row 76.
Row 85: Rep inc (row 81). *1 st inc; 29 sts.*
Row 86: Rep shift B WS (row 80).
Row 87: Rep shift C RS (row 79).
Row 88: Rep row 76.
Row 89: Rep inc, shift B RS (row 77). *1 st inc; 30 sts.*
Row 90: Rep row 76.
Row 91: Rep shift C RS (row 79).
Row 92: Rep shift B WS (row 80).
Row 93: Rep inc (row 81). *1 st inc; 31 sts (8 sts in yarn A, 14 sts in yarn B and 9 sts in yarn C).*
Row 94: Rep row 76.

Sections 1–3 have established the shawl body increases (worked on every 4th row), how to change colours at the y-markers (ITy), and introduced the way that the colours shift across the shawl by working pairs of increases and decreases.

4 WORK INCREASES, SHIFT YARNS B AND C
Throughout section 4, yarn B will continue to shift on every 3rd row, and yarn C now shifts on every 9th row. This creates a shallow curve in yarn C, and a deeper curve in yarn B. At the end of this section we will reach the narrowest point of the yarn A shape. Shawl body increases continue on 4th rows (these were established on row 1 of section 1, and are worked with yarn A as k3, slmx, M1R).

Continue to inc as set on 4th rows (the last inc row in section 3 was row 93, so the next inc will be on row 97). These increases are **not** written into the instructions due to the repeat in the shift pattern. Writing out the row numbers and marking which rows require shawl body incs is a good idea.

Row 95 (shift B and C, RS): Work in yarn A to 2 sts before y-marker, k2tog, ITy, with yarn B, k1, M1R, knit to 2 sts before y-marker, k2tog, ITy, with yarn C, k1, M1R, knit to end.
Row 96 (WS): With yarn C, k3, slmx, purl to y-marker, ITy, with yarn B, purl to y-marker, ITy, with yarn A, purl to x-marker, slmx, k3.
Row 97: Work in yarn A to y-marker, ITy, with yarn B, knit to y-marker, ITy, with yarn C, knit to end.
Row 98 (shift B, WS): With yarn C, k3, slmx, purl to y-marker, ITy, with yarn B, purl to 1 st before y-marker, M1P-R, p1, ITy, with yarn A, p2tog, purl to x-marker, slmx, k3.
Row 99: Rep row 97.
Row 100: Rep row 96.
Row 101 (shift B, RS): Work in yarn A to 2 sts before y-marker, k2tog, ITy, with yarn B, k1, M1R, knit to y-marker, ITy, with yarn C, knit to end.
Row 102: Rep row 96.
Row 103: Rep row 97.

Row 104 (shift B and C, WS): With yarn C, k3, purl to 1 st before y-marker, M1P-R, p1, ITy, with yarn B, p2tog, purl to 1 st before y-marker, M1P-R, p1, ITy, with yarn A, p2tog, purl to x-marker, slmx, k3.
Row 105: Rep row 97.
Row 106: Rep row 96.
Row 107: Rep shift B RS (row 101).
Row 108: Rep row 96.
Row 109: Rep row 97.
Row 110: Rep shift B WS (row 98).
Row 111: Rep row 97.
Row 112: Rep row 96.

Rows 113–130: Rep rows 95–112 once more. *9 sts inc; 40 sts (5 sts in yarn A, 22 sts in yarn B and 13 sts in yarn C).*

Rows 131–136: Rep rows 95–100 once more. *1 st inc; 41 sts (4 sts in yarn A, 23 sts in yarn B and 14 sts in yarn C).*

The next row has a shawl body inc and yarn B shift, but needs to be worked slightly differently than before since so few yarn A sts are remaining.

Row 137 (modified inc and shift B, RS): With yarn A, k2, ssk (removing x-marker and replacing it once ssk is worked), M1R, ITy, with yarn B, k1, M1R, knit to y-marker, ITy, with yarn C, knit to end. *1 st inc; 42 sts (4 sts in yarn A, 24 sts in yarn B and 14 sts in yarn C).*
Row 138: Rep row 96.

5 WORK INCREASES, SHIFT YARNS B AND C
At the start of section 5 yarn B shifts on 10th rows and yarn C shifts on 20th rows. From row 239, yarn B shifts on 16th rows. Shifting less frequently creates shallower curves. Standard shawl body increases continue on 4th rows throughout (the first of these will be on row 141), and are written in to the instructions.

Row 139 (RS): Work in yarn A as set to y-marker, ITy, with yarn B, knit to y-marker, ITy, with yarn C, knit to end.
Row 140 (WS): With yarn C, k3, slmx, purl to y-marker, ITy, with yarn B, purl to y-marker, ITy, with yarn A, purl to x-marker, slmx, k3.
Row 141 (inc, RS): With yarn A, k3, slmx, M1R, knit to y-marker, ITy, with yarn B, knit to y-marker, ITy, with yarn C, knit to end. *1 st inc.*
Row 142: Rep row 140.
Rows 143–146: Rep rows 139–142 once more. *1 st inc.*
Row 147 (shift B and C, RS): Work in yarn A to 2 sts before y-marker, k2tog, ITy, with yarn B, k1, M1R, knit to 2 sts before y-marker, k2tog, ITy, with yarn C, k1, M1R, knit to end.
Rows 148–150: Rep rows 140–142. *1 st inc.*
Rows 151–154: Rep rows 139–142. *1 st inc.*
Rows 155–156: Rep rows 139–140.

Row 157 (inc, shift B, RS): With yarn A, k3, slmx, M1R, knit to 2 sts before y-marker, k2tog, ITy, with yarn B, k1, M1R, knit to y-marker, ITy, with yarn C, knit to end. *1 st inc.*
Row 158: Rep row 140.

Rows 159–238: Rep rows 139–158 a further 4 times. *25 sts inc; 67 sts (19 sts in yarn A, 29 sts in yarn B and 19 sts in yarn C).*

Rows 239–250: Rep rows 139–142 a further 3 times. *3 sts inc.*
Rows 251–252: Rep rows 139–140.
Row 253: Rep inc, shift B RS (row 157). *1 st inc.*
Rows 254: Rep row 140.
Rows 255–270: Rep rows 239–254 once more. *8 sts inc; 75 sts.*

Rows 271–274: Rep rows 139–142. *1 st inc; 76 sts (26 sts in yarn A, 31 sts in yarn B and 19 sts in yarn C).*

6 COMPLETE INCREASES, INTRODUCE YARN D, SHIFT YARNS B, C AND D
Row 275 (RS): Work in yarn A to y-marker, ITy, with yarn B, knit to y-marker, ITy, with yarn C, knit to 3 sts before x-marker, k2tog, pmy, join yarn D and with yarn D, k1, M1R, slmx, k3.

Now that yarn D has been joined in, it will shift on every other row, rapidly increasing the number of yarn D stitches and decreasing the number of yarn C stitches. Yarn B shifts just twice more, and the shawl body increases are completed.

Row 276 (WS): With yarn D, k3, slmx, purl to y-marker, ITy, with yarn C, purl to y-marker, ITy, with yarn B, purl to y-marker, ITy, with yarn A, purl to x-marker, slmx, k3.
Row 277 (inc, shift D, RS): With yarn A, k3, slmx, M1R, knit to y-marker, ITy, with yarn B, knit to y-marker, ITy, with yarn C, knit to 2 sts before y-marker, k2tog, ITy, with yarn D, k1, M1R, knit to end. *1 st inc.*
Row 278: Rep row 276.
Row 279 (shift D, RS): With yarn A, k3, slmx, knit to y-marker, ITy, with yarn B, knit to y-marker, ITy, with yarn C, knit to 2 sts before y-marker, k2tog, ITy, with yarn D, k1, M1R, knit to end.

Row 280–283: Rep rows 276–279 once more. *2 sts inc; 78 sts.*
Rows 284–286: Rep rows 276–278. *1 st inc; 79 sts.*

Row 287 (shift B and D, RS): With yarn A, k3, slmx, knit to 2 sts before y-marker, k2tog, ITy, with yarn B, k1, M1R, knit to y-marker, ITy, with yarn C, knit to 2 sts before y-marker, k2tog, ITy, with yarn D, k1, M1R, knit to end.
Row 288–299: Rep rows 276–279 a further 3 times. *3 sts inc; 82 sts.*
Row 300: Rep row 276.

Row 301 (inc, shift B and D, RS): With yarn A, k3, slmx, M1R, knit to 2 sts before y-marker, k2tog, ITy, with yarn B, k1, M1R, knit to y-marker, ITy, with yarn C, k2tog, ITy, with yarn D, k1, M1R, knit to end. *1 st inc; 83 sts (31 sts in yarn A, 33 sts in yarn B, 1 st in yarn C and 18 sts in yarn D).*
Row 302 (WS): Rep row 276.
Break yarn C, leaving a tail to weave in later. This is the widest point of the shawl.

7 COMMENCE DECREASES, INTRODUCE YARN E
Row 1 (dec, join in yarn E, RS): With yarn A, k3, slmx, ssk, knit to y-marker, ITy, with yarn B, knit to 2 sts before y-marker, k2tog, slmy, join yarn E and with yarn E, k1, M1R, ITy, with yarn D, knit to end. *1 st dec; 82 sts remain.*

Now that yarn E is joined in, it will shift on every other row, thus increasing the number of yarn E stitches and decreasing the number of yarn B stitches. Shawl body decreases will occur at the beginning of every 4th row throughout sections 8–14 (first decrease was on row 1).

Row 2 (WS): With yarn D, k3, slmx, purl to y-marker, ITy, with yarn E, purl to y-marker, ITy, with yarn B, purl to y-marker, ITy, with yarn A, purl to x-marker, slmx, k3.
Row 3 (shift E): With yarn A, k3, slmx, knit to y-marker, ITy, with yarn B, knit to 2 sts before y-marker, k2tog, ITy, with yarn E, k1, M1R, knit to y-marker, ITy, with yarn D, knit to end.
Row 4: Rep row 2.
Row 5 (dec, shift E): With yarn A, k3, slmx, ssk, knit to y-marker, ITy, with yarn B, knit to 2 sts before y-marker, k2tog, ITy, with yarn E, k1, M1R, knit to y-marker, ITy, with yarn D, knit to end. *1 st dec.*
Rows 6–13: Rep rows 2–5 twice more. *3 sts dec; 79 sts remain (27 sts yarn A, 26 sts yarn B, 8 sts yarn E and 18 sts yarn D).*
Rows 14–16: Rep rows 2–4 once more. *79 sts (27 sts yarn A, 25 sts yarn B, 9 sts yarn E and 18 sts yarn D).*

8 WORK DECREASES, SHIFT YARN E
In the following section, yarn E will shift on every 4th row (the RS rows where you are NOT working shawl body decs), thus continuing to increase the number of yarn E stitches and decreasing the number of yarn B stitches. Shawl body decreases continue to occur at the beginning of every 4th row.

Row 17 (dec, RS): With yarn A, k3, slmx, ssk, knit to y-marker, ITy, with yarn B, knit to y-marker, ITy, with yarn E, knit to y-marker, ITy, with yarn D, knit to end. *1 st dec.*
Row 18 (WS): With yarn D, k3, slmx, purl to y-marker, ITy, with yarn E, purl to y-marker, ITy, with yarn B, purl to y-marker, ITy, with yarn A, purl to x-marker, slmx, k3.
Row 19 (shift E): With yarn A, knit to y-marker, ITy, with yarn B, knit to 2 sts before y-marker, k2tog, ITy, with yarn E, k1, M1R, knit to y-marker, ITy, with yarn D, knit to end.
Row 20: Rep row 18.

Rows 21–56: Rep rows 17–20 a further 9 times. *10 sts dec; 69 sts (17 sts in yarn A, 15 sts in yarn B, 19 sts in yarn E and 18 sts in yarn D).*

9 WORK DECREASES, SHIFT YARNS D AND E
In the following section, yarn E shifts on every 6th row thus increasing the number of yarn E stitches and decreasing the number of yarn B stitches. Yarn D shifts on 20th rows, thus decreasing the number of yarn D stitches, and increasing the number of yarn E stitches – this shift is worked with an increase followed by a decrease (the opposite way to the other shifts). Shawl body decreases continue on every 4th row.

Continue to dec as set (with yarn A, k3, slmx, ssk) on 4th rows (the last dec row in section 8 was row 53, so the next dec will be on row 57). These decreases are not written into the instructions due to the repeat in the shift pattern. Writing out the row numbers and marking which rows require shawl body decs is a good idea.

Row 57 (RS): Work in yarn A to y-marker, ITy, with yarn B, knit to y-marker, ITy, with yarn E, knit to y-marker, ITy, with yarn D, knit to end.
Row 58 (WS): With yarn D, k3, slmx, purl to y-marker, ITy, with yarn E, purl to y-marker, ITy, with yarn B, purl to y-marker, ITy, with yarn A, purl to x-marker, slmx, k3.
Rows 59–60: Rep rows 57–58.

Row 61 (shift E, RS): Work in yarn A to y-marker, ITy, with yarn B, knit to 2 sts before y-marker, k2tog, ITy, with yarn E, k1, M1R, knit to y-marker, ITy, with yarn D, knit to end.
Row 62: Rep row 58.

Rows 63–74: Rep rows 57–62 twice more.

Row 75 (shift D, RS): Work in yarn A to y-marker, ITy, with yarn B, knit to y-marker, ITy, with yarn E, knit to 1 st before y-marker, M1L, k1, ITy, with yarn D, ssk, knit to end.
Rows 76–80: Rep rows 58–62.
Rows 81–92: Rep rows 57–62 twice more.
Rows 93–94: Rep rows 57–58.

Row 95: Rep shift D (row 75).
Row 96: Rep row 58.
Row 97: Rep shift E (row 61).
Row 98: Rep row 58.

Rows 99–108: Rep rows 57–62 once more, then rep rows 57–60 once more. *13 sts dec; 56 sts remain (4 sts in yarn A, 7 sts in yarn B, 29 sts in yarn E and 16 sts in yarn D).*

10 WORK DECREASES, SHIFT YARNS D AND E
The next few rows have shawl body decreases and yarn D and E shifts, but they need to be worked slightly differently than before since so few yarn A sts are remaining. The shawl body decreases are written in to this section as they are not worked as previously.

Row 109 (modified dec and shift E, RS): With yarn A, k3, remove x-marker, IT, with yarn B, k2tog (removing y-marker), knit to 2 sts before y-marker, k2tog, ITy, with yarn E, k1, M1R, knit to y-marker, ITy, with yarn D, knit to end. *1 st dec; 55 sts remain. 1 x-marker and 2 y-markers remain.*
Row 110 (WS): With yarn D, k3, slmx, purl to y-marker, ITy, with yarn E, purl to y-marker, ITy, with yarn B, purl to last 3 sts, IT, with yarn A, k3.
Row 111: With yarn A, k3, IT, with yarn B, knit to y-marker, ITy, with yarn E, knit to y-marker, ITy, with yarn D, knit to end.
Row 112: Rep row 110.
Row 113 (dec): With yarn A, k2, IT, with yarn B, k2tog, knit to y-marker, ITy, with yarn E, knit to y-marker, ITy, with yarn D, knit to end. *1 st dec; 54 sts remain.*
Row 114: With yarn D, k3, slmx, purl to y-marker, ITy, with yarn E, purl to y-marker, ITy, with yarn B, purl to last 3 sts, k1, IT, with yarn A, k2.
Row 115 (modified shift D and E): With yarn A, k2, IT, with yarn B, knit to 2 sts before y-marker, k2tog, ITy, with yarn E, k1, M1R, knit to 1 st before y-marker, M1L, k1, ITy, with yarn D, ssk, knit to end.
Row 116: Rep row 114.
Row 117 (modified dec, RS): With yarn A, k1, IT, with yarn B, k2tog, knit to y-marker, ITy, with yarn E, knit to y-marker, ITy, with yarn D, knit to end. *1 st dec; 53 sts remain (1 st in yarn A, 5 sts in yarn B, 32 sts in yarn E and 15 sts in yarn D).*

Row 118 (WS): With yarn D, k3, slmx, purl to y-marker, ITy, with yarn E, purl to y-marker, ITy, with yarn B, purl to last 3 sts, k2, IT, with yarn A, k1.
Row 119: With yarn A, k1, IT, with yarn B, knit to y-marker, ITy, with yarn E, knit to y-marker, ITy, with yarn D, knit to end.
Row 120: Rep row 118. Break yarn A, leaving a tail to weave in later.
Row 121 (modified dec): With yarn B, k2tog, knit to y-marker, ITy, with yarn E, knit to y-marker, ITy, with yarn D, knit to end. *1 st dec; 52 sts remain.*
Row 122: With yarn D, k3, slmx, purl to y-marker, ITy, with yarn E, purl to y-marker, ITy, with yarn B, purl to last 3 sts, k3.
Row 123 (shift E): With yarn B, knit to 2 sts before y-marker, k2tog, ITy, with yarn E, k1, M1R, knit to y-marker, ITy, with yarn D, knit to end.
Row 124: Rep row 122.
Row 125 (modified dec): With yarn B, k2, k2tog, ITy, with yarn E, knit to y-marker, ITy, with yarn D, knit to end. *1 st dec; 51 sts remain.*
Row 126: Rep row 122.
Row 127: With yarn B, knit to y-marker, ITy, with yarn E, knit to y-marker, ITy, with yarn D, knit to end.
Row 128: Rep row 122.
Row 129 (modified dec): With yarn B, k2, IT, with yarn E, k2tog (removing y-marker), knit to y-marker, ITy, with yarn D, knit to end. *1 st dec; 50 sts remain. 1 x-marker and 1 y-marker remain.*
Row 130: With yarn D, k3, slmx, purl to y-marker, ITy, with yarn E, purl to last 3 sts, k1, IT, with yarn B, k2.
Row 131 (modified shift E): With yarn B, k1, IT, with yarn E, k2tog, M1R, knit to y-marker, ITy, with yarn D, knit to end.
Row 132: With yarn D, k3, slmx, purl to y-marker, ITy, with yarn E, purl to last 3 sts, k2, IT, with yarn B, k1. Break yarn B, leaving a tail to weave in later.
Row 133 (modified dec): With yarn E, k2tog, k2, pmx, knit to y-marker, ITy, with yarn D, knit to end. *1 st dec; 49 sts remain. 2 x-markers and 1 y-marker.*
Row 134: With yarn D, k3, slmx, purl to y-marker, ITy, with yarn E, purl to x-marker, slmx, k3.
Row 135 (shift D): With yarn E, knit to 1 st before y-marker, M1L, k1, ITy, with yarn D, ssk, knit to end.
Row 136: Rep row 134. *49 sts (35 sts in yarn E and 14 sts in yarn D).*

11 WORK DECREASES, SHIFT YARN D
In the following section the normal shawl body decreases are re-established. There are no yarn shifts at the start of this section and then yarn D only shifts every 12th row, thus decreasing the number of yarn D stitches.

Row 137 (dec, RS): With yarn E, k3, slmx, ssk, knit to y-marker, ITy, with yarn D, knit to end. *1 st dec.*
Row 138 (WS): Rep row 134.
Row 139: With yarn E, knit to y-marker, ITy, with yarn D, knit to end.
Row 140: Rep row 134.

Rows 141–156: Rep rows 137–140 a further 4 times. *5 sts dec; 44 sts remain (30 sts in yarn E and 14 sts in yarn D).*
Rows 157–164: Rep rows 137–140 twice more. *2 sts dec.*
Rows 165–166: Rep rows 137–138. *1 st dec.*
Row 167 (shift D, RS): With yarn E knit to 1 st before y-marker, M1L, k1, ITy, with yarn D, ssk, knit to end.
Row 168: Rep row 134.

Rows 169–204: Rep rows 157–168 a further 3 times. *12 sts dec; 32 sts remain (22 sts in yarn E and 10 sts in yarn D).*

12 WORK DECREASES, SHIFT AND REMOVE YARN D
In this section, shawl body decreases continue on 4th rows, and yarn D shifts on every 4th row (the RS rows where you are NOT working shawl body decs), thus decreasing the number of yarn D stitches until the yarn D shape is complete.

Row 205 (dec, RS): With yarn E, k3, slmx, ssk, knit to y-marker, ITy, with yarn D, knit to end. *1 st dec.*
Row 206 (WS): With yarn D, k3, slmx, purl to y-marker, ITy, with yarn E, purl to x-marker, slmx, k3.
Row 207 (shift D): With yarn E, knit to 1 st before y-marker, M1L, k1, ITy, with yarn D, ssk, knit to end.
Row 208: Rep row 206.
Rows 209–232: Rep rows 205–208 a further 6 times. *7 sts dec; 25 sts remain (22 sts in yarn E and 3 sts in yarn D).*
Break yarn D, leaving a tail to weave in later.

13 COMPLETE DECREASES IN YARN E ONLY
The final section is worked in yarn E only, with shawl body decreases every 4th row as established.

Row 233 (dec, RS): K3, slmx, ssk, knit to end. *1 st dec.*
Row 234 (WS): K3, slmx, purl to x-marker, slmx, k3.
Row 235: Knit.
Row 236: Rep row 234.
Rows 237–300: Rep rows 233–236 a further 16 times. *17 sts dec; 8 sts remain.*
Rows 301–302: Rep rows 233–234 once more. *1 st dec; 7 sts remain.*

Cast off all sts knitwise.

14 FINISHING
Weave in all ends but do not trim.
Soak your shawl in lukewarm water and wool wash for 20 minutes. Squeeze out excess water (but do not wring). Press between towels to dry further. Lay your shawl flat to dry, paying attention to keep the edges straight. Check that each half of the shawl is even by measuring from the centre point to the tips of the wingspan. When the shawl is completely dry, trim any remaining ends.

TECHNIQUE
PINHOLE CAST ON

Having a range of different cast-on methods in your knitting technique tool box is one of the best ways of expanding your skills. It's all too easy to learn one way to cast on and then forget that there may be other possibly superior ways of starting a project. Cast ons can be divided into many different categories and this month's method is used specifically for starting projects from the centre before working outwards. In August (page 52) we will be learning two provisional methods (where you start a project with the option of later working down from your cast-on edge).

The pinhole (or Emily Ocker's circular) cast on is a fantastically handy way of casting on a few stitches in the round. This method enables you to start knitting from the centre of a circle and is useful for working hats from the top down, socks from the toe up, and as in this month's pattern, noses! Alex the Mouse uses a pinhole cast on for his or her nose, as well as for both feet.

STEPWISE INSTRUCTIONS FOR THE PINHOLE CAST ON

i Leaving a tail long enough to weave in later, make a loop with your working yarn.

ii Hold the loop of yarn in your left hand and place a double-pointed needle (dpn) through the loop.

iii Wrap the working yarn around the needle tip as if to knit (passing underneath the needle) (3-5).

iv Pull the stitch on your needle tip through the loop of yarn.

A YEAR OF **TECHNIQUES**

v Gently tighten the stitch on your needle.

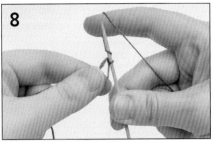

vi Wrap the working yarn around the needle tip, this time over the top of the needle first (8 and 9).

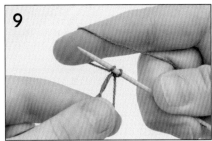

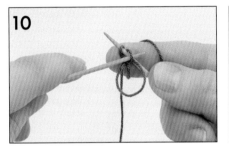

vii Use a second dpn to pull the first stitch over the second, as if to cast off.

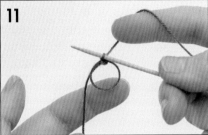

viii You now have 1 stitch on your needle.

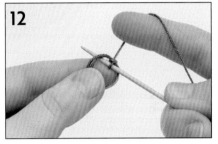

ix Put the needle tip back through the loop of yarn.

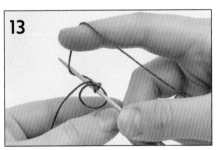

x Wrap the yarn around the tip, passing under the needle first.

xi Pull the wrap through the loop and gently tighten it.

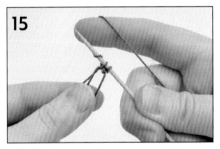

xii Wrap the working yarn round the needle, passing over the needle first.

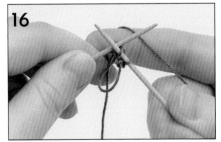

xiii Use the second dpn to pass the penultimate stitch over the last stitch, as if you were casting off.

xiv Gently tighten the stitch.

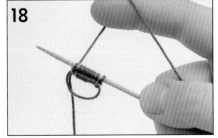

xv Repeat steps ix-xiv until you have cast on sufficient stitches.

STEPWISE INSTRUCTIONS FOR STARTING TO WORK IN THE ROUND FROM A PINHOLE CAST ON

May

i Slip your stitches onto your required number of dpns. Here we have 9 stitches and we are placing 3 stitches on each needle.

ii Once you have your stitches on the required number of needles, gently pull on the tail to tighten the pinhole.

iii Compare the wrong side of the cast-on point...

... with the right side.

iv Working with the right side towards you, and your working yarn attached to the final stitch on the previous needle, start to work in the round.

v Once you have knitted a few rounds, you can tighten the pinhole further.

NOTE

If you find that you aren't comfortable using double-pointed needles for this cast-on method, you can use a small crochet hook instead of the dpn that is held in the right hand. Once you have cast on all of your stitches, slip them from the crochet hook onto your desired needles.

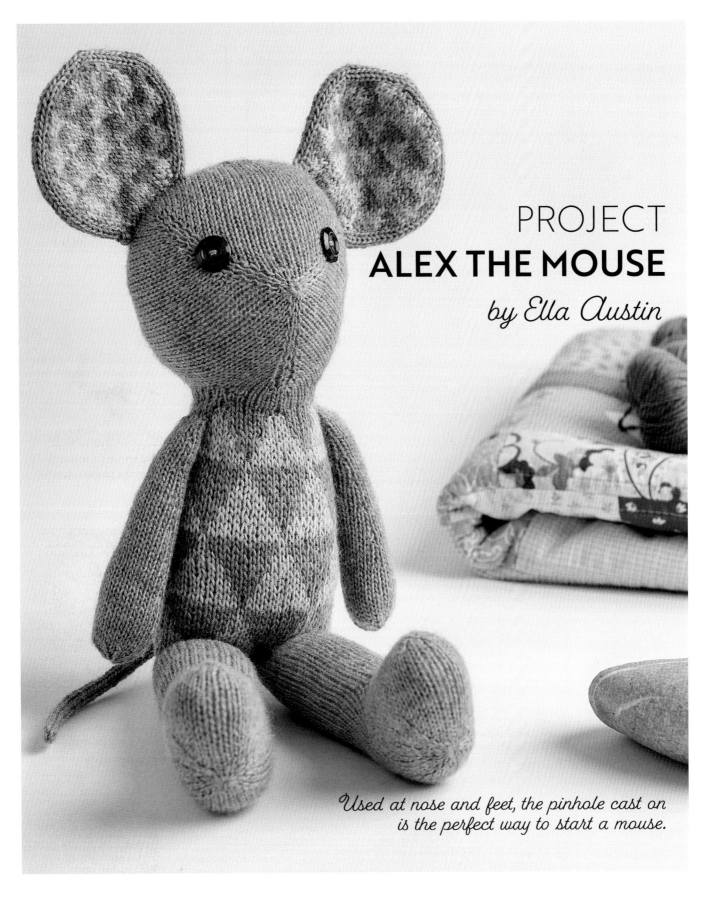

PROJECT
ALEX THE MOUSE
by Ella Austin

Used at nose and feet, the pinhole cast on is the perfect way to start a mouse.

May

SIZE
Total height: 36cm [14¼in] from ear to toe

YARN
Coop Knits Socks Yeah! (4ply weight; 75% superwash merino, 25% nylon; 212m per 50g skein)
Yarn A: Ammolite (102); 1 x 50g skein
Yarn B: Kunzite (106); 1 x 50g skein
Yarn C: Danburite (105); 1 x 50g skein

NEEDLES AND NOTIONS
1 set 2.25mm [US 1] double-pointed needles or your preferred needles for working small circumferences in the round, or size needed to match tension
2 buttons for eyes (or alternative); Stitch marker; Crochet hook (optional); Toy stuffing

TENSION
28.5 sts and 33 rounds to 10cm [4in] over stranded colourwork using 2.25mm needles, after washing and blocking
32 sts and 50 rounds to 10cm [4in] over plain stocking stitch using 2.25mm needles, after washing and blocking
Your tension needs to be tight enough that the filling doesn't poke through the stitches once Alex is stuffed.

TECHNIQUES
You will find a video tutorial on how to work an applied i-cord on our YouTube channel here: **youtu.be/Hhl5xlfeZvk**

ABBREVIATIONS
A full list of abbreviations appears on the inside back cover.

PATTERN NOTES
Alex is worked in a series of pieces as seamlessly as possible. Starting from a pinhole cast on at the nose, the head is created with a series of increases radiating out from the nose. Stitches are left on waste yarn and more are later cast on for the neck, before decreasing to a point at the back of the head. The neck is then picked up and worked down from these stitches, before commencing Alex's colourwork body. The ears are worked as 2 flat pieces, joined with an applied i-cord edge. Arms and legs are worked separately before stuffing and joining to the body.

OVERCASTING
Holding the cast-on/off edge flat with wrong sides together, start at one end of the seam, insert the needle through both sides of the piece from back to front and pull yarn through. Move along 1 stitch and insert the needle through both pieces from back to front, allowing the yarn to sit over the cast-on/off edge. Continue to the end of the piece.

CHART NOTES
All rows of chart A are read from right to left. On chart B, odd-numbered right side rows are read from right to left, and even-numbered wrong side rows are read from left to right.

MOUSE

1 NOSE
With yarn B, cast on 9 sts using the pinhole method. Distribute your sts over your needles and pm for start of round.
Round 1 and all odd-numbered rounds: Knit.
Round 2: (K1, M1L, k1, M1R, k1) 3 times. *6 sts inc; 15 sts.*
Round 4: (K2, M1L, k1, M1R, k2) 3 times. *6 sts inc; 21 sts.*

2 FRONT OF HEAD
Change to yarn A after working round 5.
Round 6: (K3, M1L, k1, M1R, k3) 3 times. *6 sts inc; 27 sts.*
Round 8: (K4, M1L, k1, M1R, k4) 3 times. *6 sts inc; 33 sts.*
Round 10: (K5, M1L, k1, M1R, k5) 3 times. *6 sts inc; 39 sts.*
Round 12: K6, M1L, (k1, M1R) twice, k11, M1L, k1, M1R, k11, (M1L, k1) twice, M1R, k6. *8 sts inc; 47 sts.*
Round 14: K7, M1L, (k1, M1R) twice, k14, M1L, k1, M1R, k14, (M1L, k1) twice, M1R, k7. *8 sts inc; 55 sts.*
Round 16: K8, M1L, (k1, M1R) twice, k17, M1L, k1, M1R, k17, (M1L, k1) twice, M1R, k8. *8 sts inc; 63 sts.*
Round 18: K9, M1L, (k1, M1R) twice, k20, M1L, k1, M1R, k20, (M1L, k1) twice, M1R, k9. *8 sts inc; 71 sts.*
Round 20: K10, M1L, (k1, M1R) twice, k23, M1L, k1, M1R, k23, (M1L, k1) twice, M1R, k10. *8 sts inc; 79 sts.*
Round 22: K11, M1L, (k1, M1R) twice, k21, knit the next 11 sts and slip them to waste yarn, k21, (M1L, k1) twice, M1R, k11. *6 sts inc; 74 live sts and 11 held sts.*
K37 to the gap at the end of the row. Keep round marker in place but work back and forth in rows for the next 6 rows, working past the marker each time.
Row 1 (WS): P74.
Row 2 (RS): K23, (M1L, k1) twice, M1R, k24, M1L, (k1, M1R) twice, k23. *6 sts inc; 80 sts.*
Row 3: P80.
Row 4: K25, (M1L, k1) twice, M1R, k26, M1L, (k1, M1R) twice, k25. *6 sts inc; 86 sts.*
Row 5: P86.
Row 6: K86, backwards loop cast on 11 sts and rejoin round. *97 sts.*
K43 to marker and continue working in rounds from this point on.

3 BACK OF HEAD
Round 1 and all odd-numbered rounds: Knit.
Round 2: (K10, k2tog) 8 times, k1. *8 sts dec; 89 sts remain.*
Round 4: (K9, k2tog) 8 times, k1. *8 sts dec; 81 sts remain.*
Round 6: (K8, k2tog) 8 times, k1. *8 sts dec; 73 sts remain.*
Round 8: (K7, k2tog) 8 times, k1. *8 sts dec; 65 sts remain.*
Round 10: (K6, k2tog) 8 times, k1. *8 sts dec; 57 sts remain.*
Round 12: (K5, k2tog) 8 times, k1. *8 sts dec; 49 sts remain.*
Round 14: (K4, k2tog) 8 times, k1. *8 sts dec; 41 sts remain.*
Round 16: (K3, k2tog) 8 times, k1. *8 sts dec; 33 sts remain.*
Round 18: (K2, k2tog) 8 times, k1. *8 sts dec; 25 sts remain.*
Round 20: (K1, k2tog) 8 times, k1. *8 sts dec; 17 sts remain.*
Round 22: (K2tog) 8 times, k1. *8 sts dec; 9 sts remain.*
Break yarn and pull through remaining sts.

4 NECK
The neck area is picked up around the opening at the base of the head.
With yarn A, pick up and knit 11 sts at back of neck, pick up and knit 7 sts along side of neck, knit across the 11 sts from waste yarn at front of neck and pick up and knit 7 sts along the other side of neck. Pm for start of round. *36 sts.*
Rounds 1–2: Knit.
Change to yarn B.
Round 3: Knit.

5 BODY
Once you have worked a few rounds of the chart pattern, turn your work inside out to ensure an even tension through your floats so that the fabric doesn't pucker. Join in yarn C.
Round 1: Work the 6 sts of row 1 of chart A 6 times.
Last round sets chart A pattern. Continue in chart A pattern, working a new row each time, changing yarns and increasing as indicated, until all 30 rows have been completed. Work chart rows 11-20 once more. *24 sts inc; 60 sts.*
Rounds 41–42: With yarn C only, knit.
Cast off all sts loosely.

6 EAR FRONTS (MAKE 2 ALIKE)
Ear fronts are worked back and forth.
With yarn C, cast on 13 sts. Join in yarn B.
Row 1 (RS): Reading from right to left, work across row 1 of chart B.
Row 2 (WS): Reading from left to right, work across row 2 of chart B.
Last 2 rows set chart B pattern. Continue in chart B pattern as set, working a new row each time, changing yarns and working increases and decreases as indicated, until all 31 rows have been worked. *4 sts dec, 9 sts remain.*
Cast off all sts purlwise.

7 EAR BACKS (MAKE 2 ALIKE)
Ear backs are worked back and forth in st st. There are slightly more rows than for the ear fronts to account for the slight difference in tension between st st and stranded colourwork.
With yarn A, cast on 13 sts.
Row 1 (RS): Knit.
Row 2 and all WS rows: Purl.
Row 3: (K1, M1L) twice, knit to last 2 sts, (M1R, k1) twice. *4 sts inc; 17 sts.*
Row 5: Rep row 3. *4 sts inc; 21 sts.*
Row 7: K1, M1L, knit to last st, M1R, k1. *2 sts inc; 23 sts.*
Rows 9 & 11: Rep row 7. *4 sts inc; 27 sts.*
Row 13: Knit.
Row 15: Rep row 7. *2 sts inc; 29 sts.*
Rows 16–24: Work in st st.
Row 25: K1, ssk, knit to last 3 sts, k2tog, k1. *2 sts dec; 27 sts remain.*
Rows 27: Rep row 25. *2 sts dec; 25 sts remain.*
Row 29: K1, (ssk) twice, knit to last 5 sts, (k2tog) twice, k1. *4 sts dec; 21 sts remain.*

May

Round 10: *K5, (M1L, k3) 5 times, k2; rep from * once more. *10 sts inc; 54 sts.*
Rounds 11-20: Knit.
Round 21: K24, ssk, k2, k2tog, knit to end. *2 sts dec; 52 sts remain.*
Round 22: Knit.
Round 23: K24, ssk, k2tog, k10, slip the last 22 sts just worked from rh needle onto waste yarn, knit to end of round. *28 sts remain on needles.*
Round 24: Knit, keeping tension tight across the gap.
Rounds 25–68: Knit.
Cast off all sts loosely.

9 ARMS (MAKE 2 ALIKE)
The arms are worked from the top down, so the pinhole cast on is not required.
With yarn A, cast on 12 sts. Distribute your sts over your needles and pm for start of round.
Rounds 1–5: Knit.
Round 6: (K1, M1L, k5) twice. *2 sts inc; 14 sts.*
Rounds 7–11: Knit.
Round 12: (K1, M1L, k6) twice. *2 sts inc; 16 sts.*
Rounds 13–17: Knit.
Round 18: (K1, M1L, k7) twice. *2 sts inc; 18 sts.*
Rounds 19–23: Knit.
Round 24: (K1, M1L, k8) twice. *2 sts inc; 20 sts.*
Rounds 25–29: Knit.
Round 30: (K1, M1L, k9) twice. *2 sts inc; 22 sts.*
Rounds 31–35: Knit.
Round 36: (K1, M1L, k10) twice. *2 sts inc; 24 sts.*
Rounds 37–46: Knit.
Round 47: (K1, k2tog) 8 times. *8 sts dec; 16 sts remain.*
Round 48: Knit.
Round 49: (K2tog) 8 times. *8 sts dec; 8 sts.*
Break yarn and pull through remaining stitches.

10 TAIL
With yarn A cast 5 sts onto a dpn.
Using a second dpn, knit across the 5 sts. *Slide the sts to the other end of the right needle without turning the work. Knit the 5 sts, giving the yarn a good tug when working the first st. Rep from * until i-cord measures 14cm [5½in].
Break yarn and pull through stitches.

11 FINISHING
Weave in all ends.
Block all pieces by soaking in cool water for 20 minutes. Gently squeeze out excess water and leave flat to dry.
When stuffing the head and body, arms and legs take the time to spread the stuffing evenly and ensure that the stuffing doesn't stretch the stitches.
Weave in all subsequent ends as you work.
Use photos as a guide for finishing.

Rows 31, 33 & 35: Rep row 29. *12 sts dec; 9 sts remain.*
Cast off all sts purlwise.

8 LEGS (MAKE 2 ALIKE)
With yarn A, cast on 12 sts using the pinhole method. Distribute your sts over your needles and pm for start of round.
Round 1: Knit.
Round 2: *(K1, M1L) twice, k1; rep from * a further 3 times. *8 sts inc; 20 sts.*
Round 3: Knit.
Round 4: *(K2, M1L) 4 times, k2; rep from * once more. *8 sts inc; 28 sts.*
Round 5: Knit.
Round 6: *(K3, M1L) twice, k2, (M1L, k3) twice; rep from * once more. *8 sts inc; 36 sts.*
Round 7: Knit.
Round 8: *(K4, M1L) twice, k2, (M1L, k4) twice; rep from * once more. *8 sts inc; 44 sts.*
Round 9: Knit.

PROJECT **ALEX THE MOUSE**

HEAD AND BODY

Stuff the head evenly and enhance the nose shaping by adding extra stuffing to this area at the end. Stuff the neck and body evenly.

Close the bottom seam using overcasting (page 30).

Sew two buttons to the face for eyes.

EARS

Join the ear front and back with an attached i-cord as follows: Hold ears together with wrong sides facing each other, and back of ear facing you. Ensure that the cast-on edges are lined up at the bottom and the cast-off edges are lined up at the top. The attached i-cord will run across the sides and top of the ear but not along the bottom (cast-on) edge.

With yarn A, cast on 3 sts onto a dpn. Starting at the right-hand side of the ear, insert the needle holding the 3 cast-on sts through the back of ear and then the front of ear and pull through a 4th stitch. *Now hold this needle in your left hand, slide the sts to the other end of the needle and pulling the yarn tight across the back, use another dpn to k2, k2tog. *3 sts remain.*

Pick up a stitch through the back and front of ear onto this dpn, as before. *4 sts.*

Rep from * picking up sts evenly around the ear (1 st picked up in each row and st of the ear), until the i-cord runs across the side, top and other side of the ear.

Break yarn and pull through last 3 sts. Seam the bottom of the ear using overcasting. Sew the ears to the top of the head firmly so that they stand up.

FEET AND LEGS

Slip the 22 sts held on waste yarn onto 2 dpns, with 11 sts on each dpn each side of the foot. With yarn A, graft the 2 sets of sts together. Sew the small gap at the end of the grafted area closed.

Stuff the feet and legs evenly.

Seam the tops of the legs using overcasting.

Sew the legs to the bottom of the body.

ARMS

Stuff the arms evenly.

Seam the tops of the arms using overcasting.

Sew the arms to the sides of the body three rows down from the neck.

TAIL

Sew the tail to the back of the body centrally between the bottom two repeats of colourwork pattern.

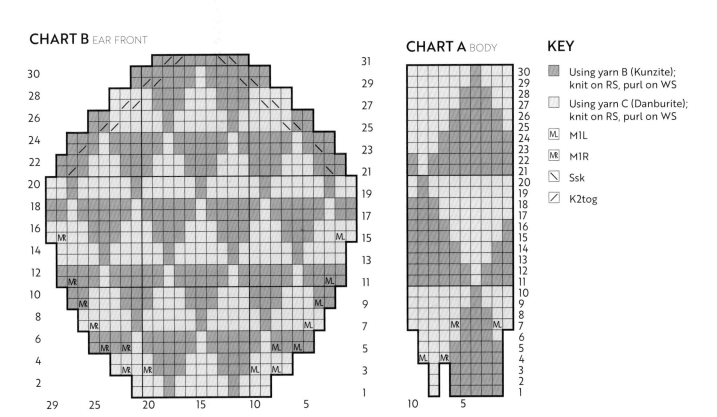

CHART B EAR FRONT

CHART A BODY

KEY

- ▨ Using yarn B (Kunzite); knit on RS, purl on WS
- ☐ Using yarn C (Danburite); knit on RS, purl on WS
- Ⓜ M1L
- Ⓜ M1R
- ◹ Ssk
- ◸ K2tog

Summer

June

TECHNIQUE **Knitted-On Edging**
PROJECT **Talmadge Cloche**
DESIGNER **Rosemary (Romi) Hill**

July

TECHNIQUE **Heel Turn**
PROJECT **Antirrhinum Socks**
DESIGNER **Rachel Coopey**

August

TECHNIQUE **Two Provisional Cast Ons**
PROJECT **Little Tern Blanket**
DESIGNER **Tin Can Knits**

TECHNIQUE
KNITTED-ON EDGING

Adding a knitted-on edging is a common construction technique used on lace shawls. It allows you to work the edging pattern perpendicular to the main pattern, at the same time casting off the main pattern stitches. For lace patterns to be really visible, they require firm stretching during blocking, and a cast-off edge is often too tight to allow the item to be stretched to its full potential. It is therefore preferable to knit your edging on, as the result is more stretchy.

Furthermore, it is a more efficient method, since you create and join the edging simultaneously, instead of having to cast off the main panel, knit a separate strip, and then sew the pieces together. It is also the case that there are many beautiful edging patterns that are worked lengthwise, creating an attractive, shaped edge. It's a simple technique, but can be tricky to visualise at first.

Your main section fabric has been created by knitting either back and forth or in the round. Your edging will be added at 90° to the main section. As each right side row of the edging is worked, it joins the edging to the main section, effectively casting off the main section stitches. A combination of single and double joins may be worked in order to create an edging that lies flat alongside the main section of fabric.

STEPWISE INSTRUCTIONS FOR WORKING A SINGLE JOIN AT THE END OF RIGHT SIDE ROWS

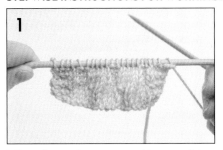

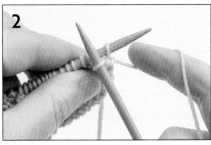

i For a flat project, you need to complete the main section with a wrong side row. Turn your work ready for the right side.

ii With the right side of your main project facing you, use a knitted on or cable cast on (page 39) to add as many stitches as directed by your pattern, to

the end of the left needle (so that they are added to the same needle as the main section stitches).

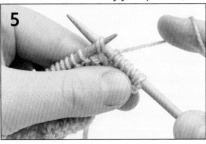

iii Work in pattern across the edging, until you have one edging stitch remaining before the main section stitches.

iv Work a left-leaning decrease (e.g. ssk or k2tog tbl) to join one edging stitch to one main section stitch.

v Without working across the main section stitches, turn your work ready for the wrong side of the edging.

vi Slip the first edging stitch purlwise (your decrease from the previous row) with your yarn in front.

vii Continue to work across the edging stitches in pattern to the end of the row.
viii Repeat steps iii–vii as directed.

Each time this join is worked at the end of a right side row, one main section stitch is effectively cast off.

STEPWISE INSTRUCTIONS FOR WORKING A DOUBLE JOIN AT THE END OF RIGHT SIDE ROWS

i–iii Work steps i–iii as for a single join.

iv Work a double decrease (sl1, k2tog, psso) to join one edging stitch to two main section stitches.

v Work remaining steps as for a single join. Each time a double join is worked, two main section stitches are cast off.

June

STEPWISE INSTRUCTIONS FOR JOINING AN EDGING TO A PROJECT WORKED IN THE ROUND
Having completed working in the round on the main section of your project, you will already have the right side of the work facing you, but your yarn is attached to your right needle.

i Without twisting it, slip the last stitch worked back to the left needle.

ii Use the knitted on or cable cast-on method to cast on as many edging stitches as directed in your pattern.

TIP
You may find it easiest to use a double-pointed needle to work the edging, leaving the main section stitches on a circular needle (or double-pointed needles if that is what you've been using).

iii Now work in pattern across the first row of the edging, until you have one edging stitch remaining before the main section stitches.

iv Work a left-leaning decrease (e.g. ssk or k2tog tbl) to join one edging stitch to one main section stitch.

v Without working across the main section stitches, turn your work ready

for the wrong side of the edging.

vi Slip the first edging stitch purlwise (your decrease from the previous row) with your yarn in front.

vii Continue to work across the edging stitches in pattern to the end of the row.

viii Repeat steps iii–vii as directed in your pattern.

Each time this join is worked at the end of a right side row, one main section stitch is effectively cast off.

You can work double joins on projects in the round in the same way as they are worked on flat projects.

STEPWISE INSTRUCTIONS FOR A KNITTED CAST ON

i Insert your right needle into the last stitch on your left needle, as if to knit.

ii Wrap the yarn round and pull through a loop (as if you were knitting).

iii Without slipping the stitch off your left needle, place the loop onto the end of the left needle.

iv Gently tighten your new stitch. Repeat steps i–iv until you have the correct number of new stitches.

STEPWISE INSTRUCTIONS FOR A CABLE CAST ON

i Insert your right needle between the last 2 stitches on your left needle.

ii Wrap the yarn round and pull through a loop.

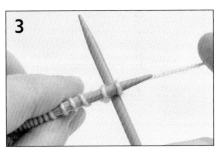

iii Place the loop on your left needle.
iv Insert your right needle between the last 2 stitches on your left needle.

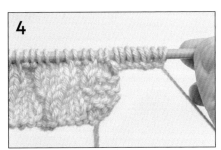

v Gently tighten the new stitch. Repeat steps ii–v until you have the correct number of new stitches (omitting step iv on your final stitch).

APPLICATIONS OF KNITTED-ON EDGINGS

This month's pattern is for a hat knitted from the top down, with a knitted-on edging creating the brim of the hat. Knitted-on edgings are very familiar in lace knitting, but there is no reason not to work a cable or other textured edging in this way. In fact, there are many, many different situations in which you might want to add a perpendicular edging to your project.

Here are a few ideas to start you off:

❖ Work a plain sock from the toe up, and then knit a lace edging on to create the cuff.
❖ Use a provisional cast on (page 52) to start a scarf and work the centre section. Then you can add matching knitted-on edgings at each end.
❖ Use a lace or cable knitted-on edging to create the collar or hem on a sweater project.

PROJECT
TALMADGE
CLOCHE

by Rosemary (Romi) Hill

An elegant cloche to see you through a rainy British summer.

SIZE
Circumference at top of knitted-on edging:
48cm [19in] unstretched
Length as finished: 21-24cm [8¼-9½in]

YARN
Fyberspates Vivacious 4ply (4ply / fingering weight; 100% superwash merino; 365m per 100g skein)
Dovestone (612); 1 x 100g skein

TENSION
25 sts and 34 rows to 10cm [4in] over lace pattern using 3mm needles, after washing and blocking

NEEDLES AND NOTIONS
1 set 3mm [US 2.5] double-pointed needles, or your preferred needles for working small circumferences in the round, or size needed to match tension
1 set 3mm [US 2.5] circular needles, 40cm [16in] long, or your preferred needles for working medium circumferences in the round, or size needed to match tension
1 set 2.75mm [US 2] double-pointed needles (will only use one dpn)
Stitch marker
Tapestry needle
2 x 2cm [⅞in] buttons
2 small clear buttons to back larger buttons

TECHNIQUES
Refer back to May's tutorial (page 26) for instructions on working the pinhole cast-on method.

ABBREVIATIONS
A full list of abbreviations appears on the inside back cover.

PATTERN NOTES
The hat is started at top with a pinhole cast on and a lace pattern is worked down to the brim. The moss stitch brim is created by knitting on an edging perpendicular to the body of the hat.

HAT

1 CAST ON
With larger needles and the pinhole method, cast on 5 sts.
Pm for start of round. To follow charted instructions, move to step 2. To follow written instructions, move to step 3.

2 CHARTED INSTRUCTIONS
Round 1: Reading from right to left, work across row 1 of chart 5 times. *5 sts inc; 10 sts.*
Last round sets chart pattern. Continue to work from chart as set until chart row 39 is complete. *110 sts inc; 120 sts.*
Now work chart rows 16–39 once more, before working chart rows 64–67.

Round 68: *K1, p1; rep from * to end of round.
Rounds 69–72: Rep round 68.

Move to step 4 on page 43 to work the brim.

3 WRITTEN INSTRUCTIONS
Round 1: (K1 tbl, yo) 5 times. *5 sts inc; 10 sts.*
Round 2: *(K1, yo, k1) all into next st, p1; rep from * to end. *10 sts inc; 20 sts.*
Round 3: *K1, p1; rep from * to end.
Round 4: *K1, yo, p1, yo, k1, p1; rep from * to end. *10 sts inc; 30 sts.*
Round 5: *K1, yo, k1, p1; rep from * to end. *10 sts inc; 40 sts.*
Round 6: *K1, yo, (p1, k1) twice, p1, yo, k1, p1; rep from * to end. *10 sts inc; 50 sts.*
Round 7: *K1, yo, (k1, p1) 3 times, k1, yo, k1, p1; rep from * to end. *10 sts inc; 60 sts.*
Round 8: *K1, yo, (k1, p1) 4 times, p1, yo, k1, p1; rep from * to end. *10 sts inc; 70 sts.*
Round 9: *K1, yo, (k1, p1) 5 times, k1, yo, k1, p1; rep from * to end. *10 sts inc; 80 sts.*
Round 10: *K1, yo, k2tog, (p1, k1) twice, yo, p1, yo, (k1, p1) twice, ssk, yo, k1, p1; rep from * to end. *10 sts inc; 90 sts.*
Round 11: *K1, yo, k2tog, (p1, k1) twice, (yo, k1, p1, k1) twice, p1, ssk, yo, k1, p1; rep from * to end. *10 sts inc; 100 sts.*
Round 12: *K1, yo, k2tog, (p1, k1) twice, yo, (p1, k1) twice, p1, yo, (k1, p1) twice, ssk, yo, k1, p1; rep from * to end. *10 sts inc; 110 sts.*
Round 13: *K1, yo, k2tog, (p1, k1) twice, yo, (k1, p1) 3 times, k1, yo, (k1, p1) twice, ssk, yo, k1, p1; rep from * to end. *10 sts inc; 120 sts.*
Round 14: *K1, k2tog, (p1, k1) twice, yo, (p1, k1) 4 times, p1, yo, (k1, p1) twice, ssk, k1, p1; rep from * to end.
Round 15: *K2tog, (p1, k1) twice, yo, (k1, p1) 5 times, k1, yo, (k1, p1) twice, ssk, p1; rep from * to end.

Round 16: *Yo, (k1, p1) twice, ssk, (k1, p1) 5 times, k1, k2tog, (p1, k1) twice, yo, p1; rep from * to end.
Round 17: *K1, yo, (k1, p1) twice, ssk, (p1, k1) 4 times, p1, k2tog, (p1, k1) twice, yo, k1, p1; rep from * to end.
Round 18: *K1, p1, yo, (k1, p1) twice, ssk, (k1, p1) 3 times, k1, k2tog, (p1, k1) twice, yo, p1, k1, p1; rep from * to end.

Round 19: *K1, p1, k1, yo, (k1, p1) twice, ssk, (p1, k1) twice, p1, k2tog, (p1, k1) twice, yo, (k1, p1) twice; rep from * to end.
Round 20: *(K1, p1) twice, yo, (k1, p1) twice, ssk, k1, p1, k1, k2tog, (p1, k1) twice, yo, (p1, k1) twice, p1; rep from * to end.
Round 21: *K1, (p1, k1) twice, yo, (k1, p1) twice, ssk, p1, k2tog, (p1, k1) twice, yo, (k1, p1) 3 times; rep from * to end.
Round 22: *Yo, (k1, p1) twice, ssk, (k1, p1) 5 times, k1, k2tog, (p1, k1) twice, yo, p1; rep from * to end.
Round 23: *K1, yo, (k1, p1) twice, ssk, (p1, k1) 4 times, p1, k2tog, (p1, k1) twice, yo, k1, p1; rep from * to end.
Round 24: *K1, p1, yo, (k1, p1) twice, ssk, (k1, p1) 3 times, k1, k2tog, (p1, k1) twice, yo, p1, k1, p1; rep from * to end.
Round 25: *K1, p1, k1, yo, (k1, p1) twice, ssk, (p1, k1) twice, p1, k2tog, (p1, k1) twice, yo, (k1, p1) twice; rep from * to end.
Round 26: *(K1, p1) twice, yo, (k1, p1) twice, ssk, k1, p1, k1, k2tog, (p1, k1) twice, yo, (p1, k1) twice, p1; rep from * to end.
Round 27: *K1, (p1, k1) twice, yo, (k1, p1) twice, ssk, p1, k2tog, (p1, k1) twice, yo, (k1, p1) 3 times; rep from * to end.
Round 28: *K1, (p1, k1) twice, k2tog, (p1, k1) twice, yo, p1, yo, (k1, p1) twice, ssk, (k1, p1) 3 times; rep from * to end.
Round 29: *(K1, p1) twice, k2tog, p1, (k1, p1, k1, yo) twice, (k1, p1) twice, ssk, (p1, k1) twice, p1; rep from * to end.
Round 30: *K1, p1, k1, k2tog, (p1, k1) twice, yo, (p1, k1) twice, p1, yo, (k1, p1) twice, ssk, (k1, p1) twice; rep from * to end.
Round 31: *K1, p1, k2tog, (p1, k1) twice, yo, (k1, p1) 3 times, k1, yo, (k1, p1) twice, ssk, p1, k1, p1; rep from * to end.
Round 32: *K1, k2tog, (p1, k1) twice, yo, (p1, k1) 4 times, p1, yo, (k1, p1) twice, ssk, k1, p1; rep from * to end.
Round 33: *K2tog, (p1, k1) twice, yo, (k1, p1) 5 times, k1, yo, (k1, p1) twice, ssk, p1; rep from * to end.

Round 34: *K1, (p1, k1) twice, k2tog, (p1, k1) twice, yo, p1, yo, (k1, p1) twice, ssk, (k1, p1) 3 times; rep from * to end.
Round 35: *(K1, p1) twice, k2tog, (p1, k1) twice, (yo, k1, p1, k1) twice, p1, ssk, (p1, k1) twice, p1; rep from * to end.
Round 36: *K1, p1, k1, k2tog, (p1, k1) twice, yo, (p1, k1) twice, p1, yo, (k1, p1) twice, ssk, (k1, p1) twice; rep from * to end.
Round 37: *K1, p1, k2tog, (p1, k1) twice, yo, (k1, p1) 3 times, k1, yo, (k1, p1) twice, ssk, p1, k1, p1; rep from * to end.
Round 38: *K1, k2tog, (p1, k1) twice, yo, (p1, k1) 4 times, p1, yo, (k1, p1) twice, ssk, k1, p1; rep from * to end.
Round 39: *K2tog, (p1, k1) twice, yo, (k1, p1) 5 times, k1, yo, (k1, p1) twice, ssk, p1; rep from * to end.

Rounds 40–63: Rep rounds 16–39.

Round 64: *K1, p1, k1, k2tog, yo, (p1, k1) 6 times, p1, yo, ssk, (k1, p1) twice; rep from * to end.
Round 65: *K1, p1, k2tog, yo, (k1, p1) 7 times, k1, yo, ssk, p1, k1, p1; rep from * to end.
Round 66: *K1, k2tog, yo, (p1, k1) 8 times, p1, yo, ssk, k1, p1; rep from * to end.
Round 67: *K2tog, yo, (k1, p1) 9 times, k1, yo, ssk, p1; rep from * to end.
Round 68: *K1, p1; rep from * to end of round.
Rounds 69–72: Rep round 68.

Move to step 4 to work the brim.

4 BRIM
KNITTED-ON EDGING

Replace last stitch worked onto left needle and cast on 15 sts using 2.75mm dpn and the knitted cast-on method (page 39). RS rows will be worked with the 2.75mm dpn and WS rows will be worked with the 3mm needle from the body of the hat.

Work 15 sts (those cast on in last step) perpendicular to body of hat as follows:

Row 1 (RS): K1 tbl twice, (k1, p1) 6 times, k2tog tbl (1 st from edging and 1 st from body).

Row 2 (WS): Sl1 wyif, (p1, k1) 6 times, k1 tbl twice.

Rep rows 1 and 2 a further 119 times, until all live body sts have been cast off.

Next row (RS): K1 tbl twice, (k1, p1) 6 times, slip last st, pick up and knit one st from edge (on top of cast-off body sts so that edging end overlaps beginning) slip both sts back onto left needle, k2tog tbl.

Next row (WS): Sl1 wyif, (p1, k1) 6 times, k1 tbl twice.
Rep RS row once more.
Work WS row while executing stretchy cast off as follows:
Work 2 sts in pattern, *replace both sts on left needle, k2tog tbl, work 1 st in pattern; rep from * to end. Fasten off.

5 FINISHING

Soak in wool wash and lay flat. Allow to dry thoroughly.

Using the photograph as a guide, fold up the edges of the hat brim and sew to hat. Sew 2cm [⅞in] buttons to the outside of the hat, and attach them to small clear buttons on the inside of the hat to stabilise the fabric. Tack down other side of the hat brim to itself.

KEY

☐ Knit

● Purl

☒ K1 tbl

◣ Ssk

◿ K2tog

○ Yarn over

⩔ (K1, yo, k1) all into same stitch

☐ Pattern repeat

CHART

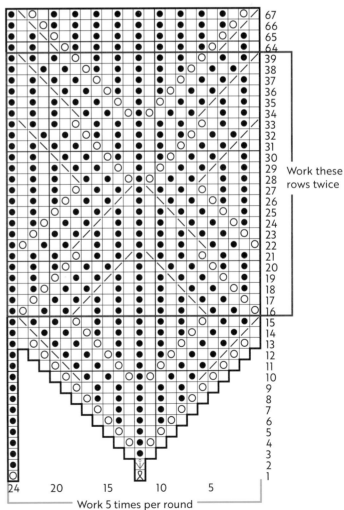

Work these rows twice

Work 5 times per round

TECHNIQUE
HEEL TURN

Turning a heel is one of the most satisfying processes in knitting. You are working a tube in one direction, and through a series of simple processes you turn a corner, allowing you to move from leg to foot. However, perhaps due to its three dimensional nature, even experienced knitters can get caught up in confusion over how a heel turn works. This tutorial will walk you through the construction of a heel flap sock, and provide you with stepwise instructions for turning the heel and returning to working in the round ready for the gusset.

Socks are among the most portable of projects. Once you have a few pairs under your belt, and you understand how the heel turn works, there is little need for instructions for a plain pair. This means you can grab a ball of sock yarn and your usual needles, and get started with minimal thought required – perfect for a project on the run.

SOCK CONSTRUCTION
The stages of making a top-down sock are as follows:

CUFF
Stitches are cast on using a stretchy method and the knitting is joined to work in the round. The cuff is then usually worked in a stretchy stitch pattern such as ribbing.

LEG
Following on from the cuff, the leg can then be worked in plain stocking stitch or with a stitch pattern.

HEEL FLAP
The heel flap generally uses half of the leg stitches. It is worked back and forth, and often uses a slipped stitch pattern to add thickness and thus durability to the back of the heel. The heel flap is worked until it is approximately square, and the first stitch of each row is often slipped to create a chain selvedge which makes picking up stitches easier when you return to working in the round.

HEEL TURN
A series of short rows are worked back and forth, to make the heel flap curve around the back of the heel, at the same time creating the wedge of fabric at the base of the heel. The short rows are worked with decreases across the turning points, thus also decreasing the number of heel stitches. This section is described in detail on the following pages.

GUSSET
Knitting in the round is then recommenced, working first across the remaining heel stitches, then picking up stitches along the side of the heel flap before working across the instep stitches and picking up down the other side of the heel flap. This returns us to knitting in the round. The gusset is then worked with decreases taking place each end of the instep stitches.

FOOT
Once the gusset decreases are complete, the foot is worked in the round until the desired foot length is achieved. For comfort, socks generally have stocking stitch on the sole (although a princess sole worked in reverse stocking stitch is also an option, as this places the smooth side of the work under the foot), with a stitch pattern worked only on the instep stitches.

TOE
Decreases are worked to shape the toe, before the stitches are either fastened off or grafted together.

STEPWISE INSTRUCTIONS FOR TURNING A HEEL

July

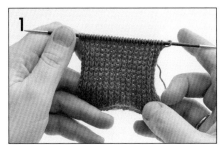

i You have worked your heel flap as described in your pattern.

ii Knit across the row as directed in your pattern.

iii Work an ssk decrease.

iv Knit 1 stitch. You will have stitches unworked at the end of the row.

NOTE

You can imagine your heel flap divided into three sets of stitches – the stitches that remain unworked at the ends of the first pair of rows, and some stitches in the centre. How many stitches you have in the centre will determine how pointy the back of your heel is, as well as how wide the base of the heel is. If you have lots of stitches in the centre, you won't work many short rows and your heel base will be wide and the curve shallow. With fewer stitches in the centre, more short rows will be worked, so the base of the heel will be narrower (as more decreases have been worked), and the back of the heel will be more curved. In the photographs there will be 10 stitches left unworked at each end of the flap, which is 32 stitches in total.

v Turn your work to the wrong side. Slip the first stitch purlwise, then purl across as directed in your pattern, before working a p2tog decrease.
vi Purl 1 stitch.

vii Turn to the right side and look at your knitting. You should have the same number of stitches unworked at each end of the row, and there should be a clear gap showing where you turned the previous row (6). In the photograph there are 10 stitches unworked at the ends, and you can clearly see the gap between the 10th and 11th stitches as counted from left to right.

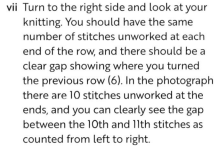

viii Slip the first stitch purlwise, then knit until you are 1 stitch before the gap.

ix Work an ssk decrease across the gap (taking the stitch before and the stitch after the gap).
x Knit 1 stitch.

xi Turn your work, leaving the remaining stitches unworked. Slip the first stitch purlwise and then purl to 1 stitch before the gap.

July

xii Purl together the next 2 stitches, thus closing the gap.

xiii Purl 1 stitch then turn, leaving the remaining stitches unworked.

Repeat steps viii–xiii until you have worked all of the heel stitches.

STEPWISE INSTRUCTIONS FOR WORKING THE GUSSET SET UP ROUND
If necessary, return your instep stitches to your needles.

i Knit across your heel stitches.

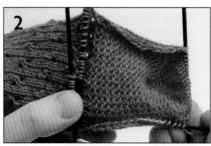

ii Use a spare double-pointed needle (dpn) to pick up the outer edge of the column of stitches down the side of the heel flap.

iii You will notice that the stitches are mounted back to front on the needle. The leading leg (or right leg) of a stitch normally sits at the front of the needle, but here the leading leg is at the rear.

iv In order to avoid gaps along the picked-up edge, I suggest knitting these stitches so that they are twisted. As the stitches are mounted back to front, you simply need to knit normally along the picked-up stitches.

v Work in pattern (refer to your sock pattern instructions) across the instep stitches.

vi Use a spare dpn to pick up stitches along the outer edge of the column of stitches along the side of the heel flap.

vii As we've worked the opposite way along the side of the heel flap, the stitches are mounted correctly.

viii In order to avoid gaps on this side of the heel flap, you now need to knit through the back loop down the side of the heel flap. This will twist the stitches and keep the join neat.

ix Now knit round across the heel stitches and up the first side of the heel flap. You are at the start of the instep, and this is your new start of the round.

x Following your pattern instructions, you will work decreases at each end of the instep stitches to shape the gusset. Once you've worked a few rounds, you should be able to see that you have turned the corner from leg to foot.

VARIATIONS ON A THEME

Rachel Coopey's lovely Antirrhinum socks which follow this tutorial will allow you to try out a basic heel turn. Then, once you have gained some confidence in turning a heel, you can play around with the stitches to find your perfect fit. Although most sock patterns have the same number of stitches for leg and foot, your feet may be narrower than your ankle. It is a simple adjustment to stop working decreases at the gusset when you've reached the number of stitches you want. You can also adjust the number of short rows to work during the heel turn – allowing you to curve the heel to best fit your foot. It is also worth bearing in mind that knitted fabric is inherently stretchy, and will be forgiving if your sock isn't absolutely perfect.

Once you have a basic set of numbers for your sock, and know how to work each section (cuff, leg, heel flap and turn, gusset, foot, toe), you can experiment with stitch patterns to create your perfect socks.

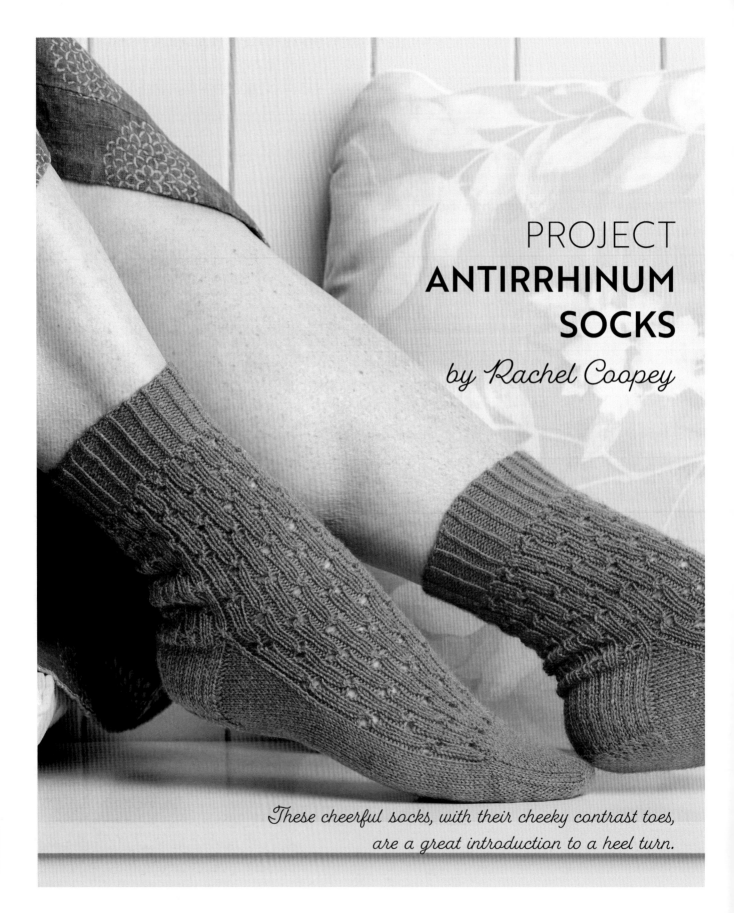

PROJECT
ANTIRRHINUM SOCKS

by Rachel Coopey

*These cheerful socks, with their cheeky contrast toes,
are a great introduction to a heel turn.*

SIZES

Small (Medium, Large)
To fit foot circumference: 20.5 (23, 25.5) cm [8 (9, 10) in]
Actual foot circumference of sock (unstretched): 16.5 (18, 19.5) cm [6½ (7¼, 7¾) in]
Length of leg to top of heel flap: 15cm [6in]
Foot length is fully adjustable within the pattern. Finished sock measures 0.5cm [¼in] less than actual foot length to ensure a good fit.

YARN

Coop Knits Socks Yeah! (4ply weight; 75% superwash merino, 25% nylon; 212m per 50g skein)
Yarn A: Ruby (116); 2 x 50g skeins
Yarn B: Iolite (109); 1 x 50g skein

NEEDLES AND NOTIONS

1 set 2.5mm [US 1.5] circular needles, 80cm [32in] long or double-pointed needles, or size needed to match tension
Stitch markers
Tapestry needle

TENSION

36 sts and 50 rounds to 10cm [4in] over st st using 2.5mm needles, after washing and blocking
44 sts and 50 rounds to 10cm [4in] over unstretched leg lace pattern using 2.5mm needles, after washing and blocking

ABBREVIATIONS

A full list of abbreviations appears on the inside back cover.

PATTERN NOTES

The charted stitch patterns are also given as written instructions. This pair of socks is designed to be mirrored.

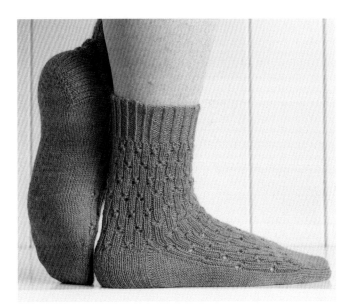

SOCK ONE

1 CUFF

With yarn A, cast on 66 (72, 78) sts. Join to work in the round, being careful not to twist. Pm for start of round.

Rib round: *K1 tbl, p2; rep from * to end.

Work rib round a further 21 times (22 rounds).
To follow charted instructions, move to step 2. To follow written instructions, move to step 3.

2 CHARTED INSTRUCTIONS

Round 1: *Reading from right to left, work 6 sts from row 1 of chart A; rep from * to end.
Last round sets chart pattern. Working next row of chart A each time, continue in pattern as set until chart A has been completed 3 times and rounds 1–6 have been worked once more (54 rounds in pattern).
Move to step 4.

3 WRITTEN INSTRUCTIONS

Round 1: *P1, k2; rep from * to end.
Round 2: *P1, yo, ssk, p1, k2; rep from * to end.
Round 3: Rep round 1.
Round 4: *P1, k2tog, yo, p1, k2; rep from * to end.
Rounds 5–9: Rep round 1.
Round 10: *P1, k2, p1, k2tog, yo; rep from * to end.
Round 11: Rep round 1.
Round 12: P1, k2, p1, yo, ssk; rep from * to end.
Rounds 13–16: Rep round 1.
Rep rounds 1–16 twice more, then work rounds 1–6 once more (54 rounds in pattern).
Move to step 4.

4 HEEL FLAP

Turn work so WS is facing. Heel flap will be worked back and forth on the next 32 (35, 38) sts, beginning with a WS row. Keep remaining 34 (37, 40) sts on needles for instep.

Row 1 (WS): Sl1 wyif, p31 (34, 37).
Row 2 (RS): *Sl1 wyib, k1; rep from * to last 0 (1, 0) st, k0 (1, 0).
Rep these 2 rows a further 14 times, then work row 1 once more.

5 HEEL TURN

Row 1 (RS): Sl1 wyib, k18 (19, 20), ssk, k1, turn, leaving remaining 10 (12, 14) sts unworked.
Row 2 (WS): Sl1 wyif, p7 (6, 5), p2tog, p1, turn, leaving remaining 10 (12, 14) sts unworked.
Row 3: Sl1 wyib, knit to 1 st before gap, ssk, k1, turn.
Row 4: Sl1 wyif, purl to 1 st before gap, p2tog, p1, turn.
Rep last 2 rows a further 4 (5, 6) times. All heel sts have been worked. *20 (21, 22) heel sts remain.*

To follow charted instructions, move to step 6. To follow written instructions, move to step 7.

6 GUSSET – CHARTED INSTRUCTIONS

Begin working in the round again as follows:

Set-up round: Sl1 wyib, k19 (20, 21), pick up and knit 16 sts along edge of heel flap (1 stitch in each slipped stitch along edge of flap);

Work across instep sts as follows: reading from right to left, work 6 outlined sts from row 1 of chart B (C, B) 5 (6, 6) times, then work final 4 (1, 4) sts of chart; pick up and knit 16 sts along edge of heel flap, k36 (37, 38). Place marker for new start of round (at start of instep sts). *86 (90, 94) sts.*

Round 1: Reading from right to left, work 6 outlined sts from row 2 of chart B (C, B) 5 (6, 6) times, then work final 4 (1, 4) sts of chart, ssk, k to 2 sts before end of round, k2tog. *2 sts dec.*

Round 2: Reading from right to left, work 6 outlined sts from row 3 of chart B (C, B) 5 (6, 6) times, then work final 4 (1, 4) sts of chart, knit to end.

Working next row of chart each time and repeating chart as required, rep these 2 rounds a further 9 (8, 7) times. *20 (18, 16) sts dec; 66 (72, 78) sts remain.*

You should now have 34 (37, 40) sts on instep and (32, 35, 38) sts on sole.

Move to step 8.

7 GUSSET – WRITTEN INSTRUCTIONS

Begin working in the round again as follows:

Set-up round: Sl1 wyib, k19 (20, 21), pick up and knit 16 sts along edge of heel flap (1 stitch in each slipped stitch along edge of flap); work across instep sts as follows: (p1, k2) 11 (12, 13) times, p1, pick up and knit 16 sts along edge of heel flap, k36 (37, 38). Place marker for new start of round (at start of instep sts). *86 (90, 94) sts.*

Next round (dec): Work round 1 of instep pattern (see below) across 34 (37, 40) instep sts, ssk, knit to last 2 sts, k2tog. *2 sts dec.*

Next round: Work round 2 of instep pattern (see below) across 34 (37, 40) instep sts, knit to end.

Working next row of instep pattern each time and repeating instep pattern as required, rep these 2 rounds a further 9 (8, 7) times. *20 (18, 16) sts dec; 66 (72, 78) sts remain.*

INSTEP PATTERN

Note: Round numbers here do not match chart row numbers.

Rounds 1 & 2: (P1, k2) 11 (12, 13) times, p1.

Round 3: (P1, k2, p1, k2tog, yo) 5 (6, 6) times, p1, k2 (0, 2), p1 (0, 1).

Round 4: Rep round 1.

Round 5: (P1, k2, p1, yo, ssk) 5 (6, 6) times, p1, k2 (0, 2), p1 (0, 1), knit to end.

Rounds 6–10: Rep round 1.

Round 11: (P1, yo, ssk, p1, k2) 5 (6, 6) times, p1, (yo, ssk, p1) 1 (0, 1) time.

Round 12: Rep round 1.

Round 13: (P1, k2tog, yo, p1, k2) 5 (6, 6) times, p1, (k2tog, yo, p1) 1 (0, 1) time.

Rounds 14–16: Rep round 1.

You should now have 34 (37, 40) sts on instep and (32, 35, 38) sts on sole.

Move to step 8.

8 FOOT

Work as set (pattern on instep and st st on sole) until the sock measures 5 (5.5, 6) cm [2 (2¼, 2¼) in] less than the desired foot length.

9 TOE

With yarn B:

Set-up round: K1, ssk, k28 (31, 34), k2tog, knit to end. *2 sts dec; 64 (70, 76) sts remain; 32 (35, 38) sts each on instep and sole.*

Round 1: Knit.

Round 2: K1, ssk, k26 (29, 32), k2tog, k1, pm, k1, ssk, knit to last 3 sts, k2tog, k1. *4 sts dec; 60 (66, 72) sts remain.*

Round 3: Knit.

Round 4: *K1, ssk, k to 3 sts before marker, k2tog, k1, slm; rep from * once more. *4 sts dec.*

Rep last 2 rounds a further 9 (10, 11) times. *40 (44, 48) sts dec; 20 (22, 24) sts remain.*

Cut yarn, leaving a 30cm [12in] tail. Graft sts together using Kitchener stitch. Weave in ends.

SOCK TWO

10 CUFF

Work as Sock One (step 1). To follow charted instructions, move to step 11. To follow written instructions, move to step 12.

11 LEG – CHARTED INSTRUCTIONS

Round 1: *Reading from right to left, work 6 sts from row 9 of chart A; rep from * to end.

Last round sets chart pattern. Working next row of chart A each time, continue in pattern as set until rounds 9–16 of chart A have been completed and rounds 1–16 have been worked twice and rounds 1–14 have been worked once more (54 rounds).

Move to step 13.

12 LEG – WRITTEN INSTRUCTIONS

Round 1: *P1, k2; rep from * to end.

Round 2: *P1, k2, p1, k2tog, yo; rep from * to end.

Round 3: Rep round 1.

Round 4: P1, k2, p1, yo, ssk; rep from * to end.

Rounds 5–9: Rep round 1.

Round 10: *P1, yo, ssk, p1, k2; rep from * to end.
Round 11: Rep round 1.
Round 12: *P1, k2tog, yo, p1, k2; rep from * to end.
Rounds 13–16: Rep round 1.
Rep rounds 1–16 twice more, then work rounds 1–6 once more (54 rounds in pattern).
Move to step 13.

13 HEEL
Work as Sock One (steps 4 and 5). To follow charted instructions, move to step 14. To follow written instructions, move to step 15.

14 GUSSET – CHARTED INSTRUCTIONS
Begin working in the round again as follows:
Set-up round: Sl1 wyib, k19 (20, 21), pick up and knit 16 sts along edge of heel flap (1 stitch in each slipped stitch along edge of flap);
Work across instep sts as follows: reading from right to left, work 6 outlined sts from row 9 of chart B (C, B) 5 (6, 6) times, then work final 4 (1, 4) sts of chart; pick up and knit 16 sts along edge of heel flap, k36 (37, 38). Place marker for new start of round (at start of instep sts). *86 (90, 94) sts.*

Round 1: Reading from right to left, work 6 outlined sts from row 10 of chart B (C, B) 5 (6, 6) times, then work final 4 (1, 4) sts of chart, ssk, k to 2 sts before end of round, k2tog. *2 sts dec.*
Round 2: Reading from right to left, work 6 outlined sts from row 11 of chart B (C, B) 5 (6, 6) times, then work final 4 (1, 4) sts of chart, knit to end.
Working next row of chart each time and repeating chart as required, rep these 2 rounds a further 9 (8, 7) times. *20 (18, 16) sts dec; 66 (72, 78) sts remain.*

You should now have 34 (37, 40) sts on instep and (32, 35, 38) sts on sole.
Move to step 16.

15 GUSSET – WRITTEN INSTRUCTIONS
Begin working in the round again as follows:
Set-up round: Sl1 wyib, k19 (20, 21), pick up and knit 16 sts along edge of heel flap (1 stitch in each slipped stitch along edge of flap); work across instep sts as follows: (p1, k2) 11 (12, 13) times, p1, pick up and knit 16 sts along edge of heel flap, k36 (37, 38). Place marker for new start of round (at start of instep sts). *86 (90, 94) sts.*

Next round (dec): Work round 9 of instep pattern (opposite) across 34 (37, 40) instep sts, ssk, knit to last 2 sts, k2tog. *2 sts dec.*
Next round: Work round 10 of instep pattern (opposite) across 34 (37, 40) instep sts, knit to end.
Working next round of instep pattern each time and repeating instep pattern as required, rep these 2 rounds a further 9 (8, 7) times. *20 (18, 16) sts dec; 66 (72, 78) sts remain.*

You should now have 34 (37, 40) sts on instep and (32, 35, 38) sts on sole.
Move to step 16.

16 FOOT AND TOE
Work as Sock One (steps 8 and 9).

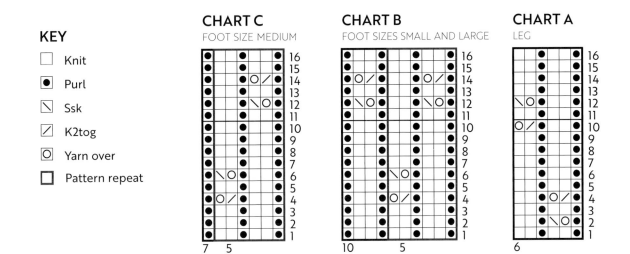

KEY
☐ Knit
⊙ Purl
◲ Ssk
⊡ K2tog
⊙ Yarn over
☐ Pattern repeat

CHART C
FOOT SIZE MEDIUM

CHART B
FOOT SIZES SMALL AND LARGE

CHART A
LEG

TECHNIQUE
TWO PROVISIONAL CAST ONS

Few things in knitting are as versatile as a provisional cast on. It allows you to get started on a project without really needing to commit to how things will end up. If you want to get going on a sweater, but haven't decided how long it will be, or what type of edging you fancy, use a provisional cast on and off you go! If you aren't sure if you have enough yarn to work the whole project in one colour, you might use a provisional cast on, and then decide later whether you need to use a contrast for the trims. But provisional cast ons aren't just handy for those indecisive moments, they also allow you to work your knitting in two directions.

Many stitch patterns have an element of direction about them. For example, a lace pattern will frequently cause the fabric to undulate in a particular direction. If you wish to make a symmetrical scarf with a stitch pattern of this sort, you would need to use a provisional cast on at the centre and then work each side out from the middle. In this way both ends of the scarf would be identical. Alternatively, a provisional cast on at one end of a strip of knitting will allow you to join the cast-on and cast-off edges at the end of the project. There are endless possibilities for ways in which this type of cast on can allow you to take your knitting in different directions.

In this tutorial you will find full instructions for two different provisional cast-on methods: the crochet provisional cast on and Judy's Magic Cast On.

The crochet method is an excellent workhorse method. It places a waste yarn crochet chain at the start of your knitting, and later on you can "unzip" the waste yarn edge to reveal live stitches in your main yarn. Either the crochet method, or Judy's Magic Cast On for a stocking stitch or textured project are suitable for this month's beautiful blanket pattern designed by Tin Can Knits.

STEPWISE INSTRUCTIONS FOR A CROCHET PROVISIONAL CAST ON

You will need a length of waste yarn (I use a mercerised cotton as it won't stick to your working yarn), a crochet hook (size isn't important as long as the hook isn't too small for your waste yarn) and your knitting needle. ➤

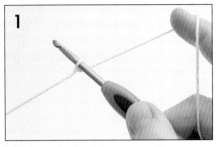

i Make a slip knot in your waste yarn and place it on a crochet hook.

ii Hold the crochet hook over your knitting needle and pass the waste yarn under the needle.

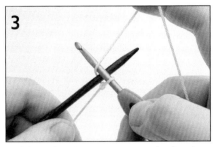

iii Wrap the waste yarn over the hook.

iv Pull the loop through the slip knot on the crochet hook. You now have 1 stitch on your knitting needle.

v Pass the waste yarn under the knitting needle and over the crochet hook.

vi Pull the loop through the stitch on the crochet hook.

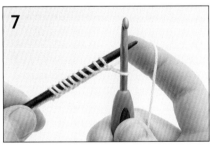

Repeat steps v and vi until you have sufficient stitches on your knitting needle.

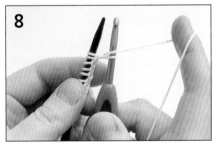

Create a chain to indicate which end of the crochet chain to unzip, as follows:
vii Wrap the yarn around the hook only.

viii Pull the yarn through the stitch on the hook. Repeat steps vii and viii until you have a short chain that is not attached to the knitting needle (5 or 6 chains is plenty).

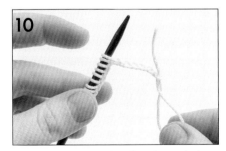

ix Cut the yarn and pull it through the final stitch.

x Change to your main yarn and work across the first row as described in your pattern.

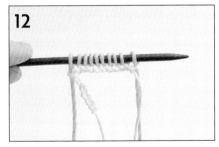

xi Having knitted the first row in main yarn you can now continue to work the pattern as instructed.

STEPWISE INSTRUCTIONS FOR UNZIPPING A CROCHET PROVISIONAL CAST ON

i Once you have worked as far as you need to, your pattern will tell you to "unzip" your provisional cast-on edge, removing the waste yarn, and to place the live stitches on a needle.

ii Locate the end of the free crochet chain, and pull the end of the waste yarn through the final loop on the chain.

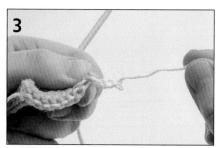

iii Once the final stitch is free, you can gently pull on the end and the chain will unravel.

iv Have your knitting needle ready and pick up the first stitch revealed in the main yarn.

v As you gently pull out the waste yarn, pick up the stitches revealed. If you're worried about dropping a stitch, you can pick up the stitch before you pull out the waste yarn (as you would pick up a stitch elsewhere in your knitting).

vi The final stitch in the row will be the point where the yarn moved up to work the second row of knitting and you may need to pull the end of the waste yarn out of this stitch.

vii Now that you have all of your main yarn stitches safely on your needles, you can continue to follow your pattern.

JUDY'S MAGIC CAST ON

What do you do if there's no crochet hook in your knitting bag, or you don't have any waste yarn to hand? Judy's Magic Cast On is a great alternative method. It's always handy to have more than one option in your provisional cast-on collection!

Judy's Magic Cast On isn't normally considered as a provisional method, but rather a way of starting closed tubes, like the toes of toe-up socks. However, it is highly versatile and particularly in combination with a set of interchangeable needles, where the stitches remaining at the cast-on edge can be left on a stoppered cable, ready to be used later. The first method here is the provisional method required for the beautiful Little Tern Blanket designed by Tin Can Knits. It is followed by methods for using Judy's Magic Cast On for a garter stitch project, and for the closed base of a tube.

STEPWISE INSTRUCTIONS FOR USING JUDY'S MAGIC CAST ON FOR A STOCKING STITCH OR TEXTURED PROJECT

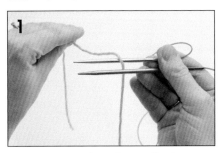

i Hold two sets of circular needles in your right hand with the tips pointing to the left. Place your yarn over the rear needle, with the tail hanging behind and the yarn attached to the ball passing between the needles. In the photos the silver needle is the rear needle, and is an interchangeable needle (these are the stitches that will remain at the cast-on edge of your knitting), and the brass needle is in front (your main working needle).

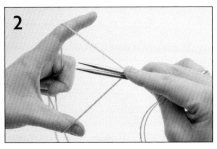

ii Use your right index finger to hold the yarn over the rear needle, and use your little, ring and middle fingers of your left hand to hold both the tail and the working yarn. Pass the tail end of the yarn over your index finger, and the working yarn over your thumb. This is very similar to how you hold yarn for a long-tail cast on, with the positions of the tail and working yarn reversed.

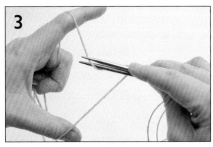

iii Use your right hand to move the needle tips under the tail end of the yarn, so that the tail goes over the front needle and down between the needles (this is as if you were drawing a clockwise circle with the tips of your needles).

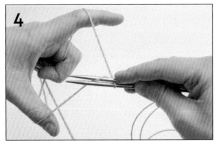

iv Gently pull to tighten the first stitch on the front needle, before moving the needle tips under the working yarn, over the rear needle and back down between the needles (this is as if you were drawing an anti-clockwise circle with the tips of your needles).

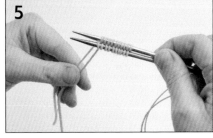

Gently tighten your stitch.
Repeat steps iii and iv as many times as required, ending on a step iii. You will usually work the same number of stitches on the front and rear needles. The photograph shows 10 stitches cast on to each needle.

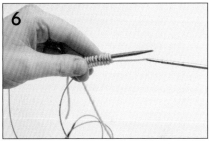

v Rotate your needles through 180°, so that the tips are now pointing to the right (don't turn them over – the purl bumps remain at the back of the work). Gently pull the stitches on what was the rear needle off the needle tip and onto the cable part of the circular needle.

vi Pick up the free tip of your main working needles (the front needles previously), and work across the first row of stitches according to your pattern. Here the first row has been worked in a k2, p2 pattern.

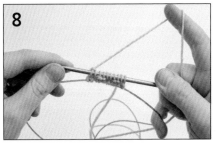

Continue to work from the pattern instructions for the main part of the knitting, before returning later to the cast-on stitches. For convenience, if you are using interchangeable needles at the cast-on edge, you can join the ends, or

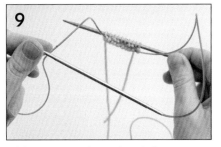

add stoppers, to keep the stitches on the cable while you work the rest of the project. When you come to knit across the cast-on edge, remove the join or stoppers, and replace the needle tips as required.

STEPWISE INSTRUCTIONS FOR USING JUDY'S MAGIC CAST ON FOR A GARTER STITCH PROVISIONAL CAST ON

While we're showing you how to do Judy's Magic Cast On, here are a couple of other ways this method can be used. They will come in handy for future projects.

i Hold two sets of circular needles in your right hand with the needle tips pointing to the left. Place your yarn over the rear needle, with the tail hanging behind the needle, and the yarn attached to the ball passing between the needles. In the

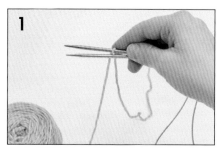

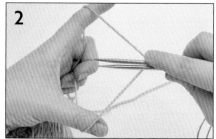

photographs the brass needle is the rear needle and the silver needle is in front. If you have a set of interchangeable needles, ensure you are using them for the front needle, as these are the stitches that will remain at the cast-on edge of your knitting.

ii Use your right index finger to hold the yarn over the rear needle, and use your little, ring and middle fingers of your left hand to hold both the tail and the working yarn. Pass the tail end of the yarn over your index finger, and the working yarn over your thumb. This is very similar to how you hold yarn for a long-tail cast on, with the positions of the tail and working yarn reversed.

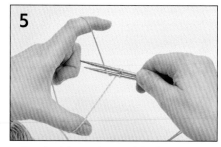

iii Use your right hand to move the needle tips under the tail end of the yarn, so that the tail goes over the front needle and down between the needles (this is as if you were drawing a clockwise circle with the tips of your needles).

iv Gently pull to tighten the first stitch on the front needle, before moving the needle tips under the working yarn, over the rear needle and back down between the needles (this is as if you were drawing an anti-clockwise circle with the tips of your needles).

v Gently tighten the stitch before passing the needle tips under the tail yarn, taking the tail over the front needle and back down between the needles.

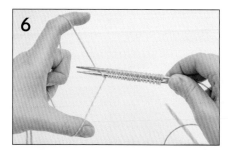

Repeat steps iv and v as many times as required. You will usually work the same number of stitches on the front and rear needles. The photograph shows 20 stitches cast on to each needle.

vi Turn your knitting upside down, so that you can see the first garter stitch ridge at the front of your work, and the needle tips are pointing to the right.

vii Carefully pull the needle closest to you, so that the front set of stitches moves on to the cable section of the (interchangeable) circular needle.

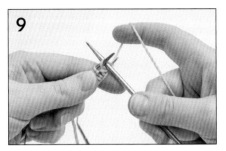

viii You will notice that the stitches are mounted back to front (with the leading leg at the rear of the needle). Holding the tail securely, use the free end of the rear needle and the working yarn to knit through the back loops across all stitches.

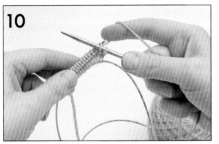

ix When you reach the end of the row, turn your work and knit across the next (and all following rows) as normal.

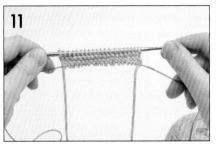

x Once you have worked a few rows, you will see that you have a set of stitches at the cast-on edge that are waiting to be worked later. You may choose to slip these stitches to waste yarn, or to remove the needle tips and replace them with stoppers (if you are using interchangeable needles), while you work the rest of your project.

STEPWISE INSTRUCTIONS FOR HOW TO WORK JUDY'S MAGIC CAST ON FOR THE CLOSED BASE OF A TUBE

This is the method required for starting a toe up sock, or the closed base of a bag.

i Hold two sets of circular needles in your right hand with the needle tips pointing to the left. Place your yarn over the rear needle, with the tail hanging behind the needle, and the yarn attached to the ball

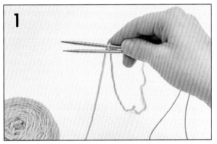

passing between the needles. In the photographs the brass needle is the rear needle and the silver needle is in front.

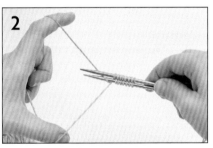

ii–v Work steps ii–v as for the garter stitch provisional cast on above. Repeat steps iv and v as many times as required. You will usually work the same number of stitches on the front and rear needles. The photograph shows 8 stitches cast on to each needle.

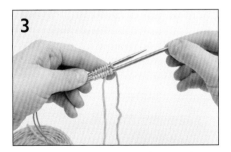

To start working in the round, grasp the tail and working yarn so that the final stitches don't slip off the needles, and rotate the needle tips through 180°. They will now be pointing towards the right.

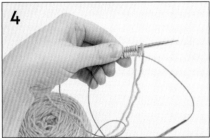

vi Pull the needle tip of what was the rear needle (but is now in the front) so that the stitches are sitting on the cable instead of the tip. This makes the first row of stitches much easier to work.

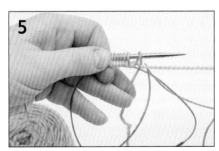

vii Holding the tail of yarn down, make sure that your working yarn is passing over the tail to secure it before you use the working yarn to knit the first stitch on the needle.

August

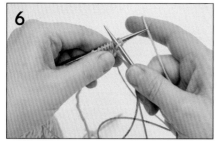

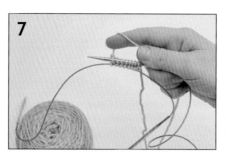

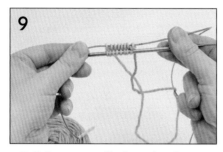

viii Using the free needle tip from the same circular needle, knit across the stitches on what is now the rear needle (6 and 7).

ix Carefully pull the front needle so that the stitches are returned to the needle tip, with the end of the tip next to the working yarn.

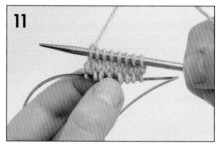

x Pull the rear needle tip so that the stitches you have just knitted are now sitting on the cable rather than the needle.

xi Turn your work through 180° again, and use the free end of the same circular needle to knit across the stitches, this time working through the back loop, as these stitches are mounted back to front (with the leading leg of each stitch at the rear). You only need to work through the back loops on the very first time you knit these stitches.

xii At the end of this needle tip you can start to see that you are working in the round from a closed base.

APPLICATIONS OF PROVISIONAL CAST ONS
Now that you have a few ways of starting a project provisionally, why not combine a provisional cast on with last month's technique, adding a knitted-on edging? This is a great way to personalise a standard pattern. You could add an edging to a sweater, socks or even a pair of mittens. There are so many possibilities!

PROJECT
LITTLE TERN BLANKET
by Tin Can Knits

A versatile blanket that's sized from baby to big, featuring textured and lace chevrons, like a little tern's tail.

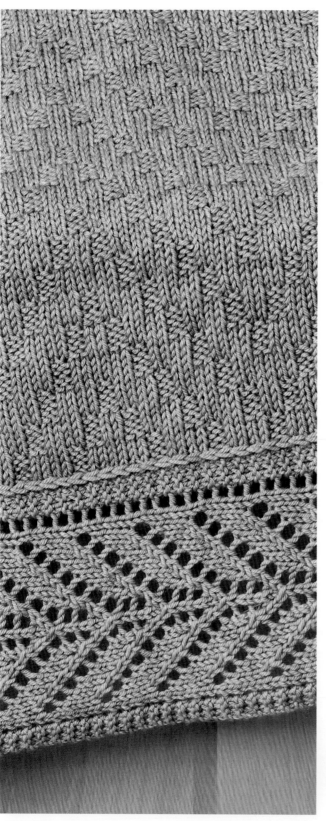

August

SIZES

Small (Medium, Large, XL)
Width: 58 (66.5, 75.5, 84.5) cm [22¾ (26¼, 29¾, 33¼) in]
Length: 94.5 (99, 103.5, 117) cm [37¼ (39, 40¾, 46) in]
Shown in smallest size.

YARN

Fyberspates Vivacious DK (DK weight; 100% superwash
merino; 230m per 115g skein)
Pebble Beach (814); 3 (4, 4, 5) x 115g skeins

NEEDLES AND NOTIONS

1 set 4.5mm [US 7] circular needles, 80cm [32in] long, or size
needed to match tension
Stitch markers
Crochet hook and waste yarn for crochet provisional cast on
or spare 4.5mm [US 7] circular needles, 80cm [32in] long for
Judy's Magic Cast On

TENSION

18 sts and 27 rows to 10cm [4in] over blanket body pattern
stitch pattern (chart A or B), after washing and blocking
The 26-stitch wide edge lace panel (charts C and D) measures
14cm [5½in] wide, after washing and blocking

TECHNIQUES

Refer back to June's tutorial (page 37) for instructions on
working the knitted-on edging.

ABBREVIATIONS

A full list of abbreviations appears on the inside back cover.

PATTERN NOTES

The blanket body is knitted first, starting from a provisional
cast on. Once the body is complete, the first lace edge is
worked as a knitted-on border. Finally, the second lace
edge is worked as a knitted-on border over the stitches
provisionally cast on.

 As the recommended yarn is hand-dyed, it is a good
idea to work with 2 skeins at the same time throughout the
body of the blanket, working 2 row stripes so that any small
differences in dyelot are disguised. The two edging strips can
be worked from a single skein of yarn.

 To adjust the length of your blanket, work more or fewer
rows in pattern, ending with a WS row 4, 8 or 12, keeping in
mind that the blanket edging will add 14cm [5½in] to each
end of the blanket, making a total 28cm [11in] additional
length.

CHART NOTES

Odd-numbered, right side rows are read from right to left.
Even-numbered, wrong side rows are read from left to right.
Each 8-row repeat of charts C and D (lace edging charts) casts
off 6 blanket body stitches.

BLANKET

1 CAST ON WITH JUDY'S MAGIC CAST ON

Move to step 2 for a crochet provisional cast on.

Cast on 104 (120, 136, 152) sts using 2 circular needles with Judy's Magic Cast On (you will have 104 (120, 136, 152) sts on each circular needle tip).

Rotate your needles through 180°, so that the tips are now pointing to the right (don't turn them over – the purl bumps remain at the back of the work).

Pick up the free needle tip of your main working needles (which were the front needles previously) ready to work to blanket body. Once you have worked a few rows, if you are using interchangeable needles, you can remove the needle tips from the cast-on edge, and replace them with stoppers, or you may wish to slip your cast-on sts to waste yarn.

Move to step 3 for charted instructions or step 4 for written instructions.

2 CAST ON WITH A CROCHET PROVISIONAL CAST ON

Using waste yarn, a crochet hook and a 4.5mm circular needle, cast on 104 (120, 136, 152) sts.

Change to main yarn and purl 1 (WS) row.

Move to step 3 for charted instructions or step 4 for written instructions.

3 BLANKET BODY - CHARTED INSTRUCTIONS

Row 1 (RS): Work across row 1 of chart A (B, A, B), repeating marked section 3 (3, 4, 4) times in total.

Row 2 (WS): Work across row 2 of chart A (B, A, B), repeating marked section 3 (3, 4, 4) times in total.

Last 2 rows set chart A (B, A, B) pattern. Working next row of chart A (B, A, B) each time, continue in pattern as set until chart A (B, A, B) has been completed 15 (16, 17, 20) times (180 (192, 204, 240) rows in pattern).

It can be helpful to place markers to separate the 32-st panels, as indicated by the red boxes on the chart.

Move to step 5.

4 BLANKET BODY - WRITTEN INSTRUCTIONS

SIZES SMALL AND LARGE ONLY

Row 1 (RS): K3, p1, *p1, (k4, p2) twice, k6, (p2, k4) twice, p1; rep from * to last 4 sts, p1, k3.

Row 2 (WS): K4, *k1, (p4, k2) twice, p6, (k2, p4) twice, k1; rep from * to last 4 sts, k4.

Rows 3 & 4: Rep rows 1 & 2.

Row 5: K4, *k1, (p2, k4) twice, p2, k2, p2, (k4, p2) twice, k1; rep from * to last 4 sts, k4.

Row 6: K3, p1, *p1, (k2, p4) twice, k2, p2, k2, (p4, k2) twice, p1; rep from * to last 4 sts, p1, k3.

Rows 7 & 8: Rep rows 5 & 6.

Row 9: K4, *k3, (p2, k4) 4 times, p2, k3; rep from * to last 4 sts, k4.

Row 10: K3, p1, *p3, (k2, p4) 4 times, k2, p3; rep from * to last 4 sts, p1, k3.

Rows 11 & 12: Rep rows 9 & 10.

SIZES MEDIUM AND XL ONLY

Row 1 (RS): K3, p1, *p1, (k4, p2) twice, k6, (p2, k4) twice, p1; rep from * to last 20 sts, p1, (k4, p2) twice, k7.

Row 2 (WS): K3, p4, (k2, p4) twice, k1, *k1, (p4, k2) twice, p6, (k2, p4) twice, k1; rep from * to last 4 sts, k4.

Rows 3 & 4: Rep rows 1 & 2.

Row 5: K4, *k1, (p2, k4) twice, p2, k2, p2, (k4, p2) twice, k1; rep from * to last 20 sts, k1, (p2, k4) 3 times, k1.

Row 6: K3, p2, (k2, p4) twice, k2, p1, *p1, (k2, p4) twice, k2, p2, k2, (p4, k2) twice, p1; rep from * to last 4 sts, p1, k3.

Rows 7 & 8: Rep rows 5 & 6.

Row 9: K4, *k3, (p2, k4) 4 times, p2, k3; rep from * to last 20 sts, k3, (p2, k4) twice, p2, k3.

Row 10: K5, (p4, k2) twice, p3, *p3, (k2, p4) 4 times, k2, p3; rep from * to last 4 sts, p1, k3.

Rows 11 & 12: Rep rows 9 & 10.

ALL SIZES

Rep last 12 rows a further 14 (15, 16, 19) times (180 (192, 204, 240) rows in pattern).

It can be helpful to place markers to separate the 32-st repeated sections.

Move to step 5.

5 BLANKET EDGING

The lace edging is worked at 90° to the blanket body. As you work rows of the lace edge, you gradually decrease the blanket body stitches, effectively casting off one or two stitches with each RS row of the lace edging.

Having completed the blanket body with a WS row, you have the RS of the work facing, and all of the stitches on the left needle.

With RS facing, using the cable method (page 39), loosely cast on an additional 26 sts to the left needle.

Row 1 (RS): K25, ssk (this works the last of the newly cast-on sts together with the first of the blanket body sts), turn.

Row 2 (WS): Sl1 (the ssk from previous row), knit to end.

Rep last 2 rows a further 3 (2, 4, 3) times. *126 (143, 157, 174) sts total; 26 edge sts plus 100 (117, 131, 148) remaining body sts.*

Move to step 6 for charted instructions or step 7 for written instructions.

6 CHARTED INSTRUCTIONS

In the following section, for every 8-row repeat of charts C and D, 6 body stitches are decreased.

Next row (RS): Work across row 1 of chart C. *2 body sts dec.*

Next row (WS): Work across row 2 of chart C.

Last 2 rows set chart C pattern. Working next row of chart C each time, continue in pattern as set until chart C has been completed 11 (11, 13, 16) times (88 (88, 104, 128) rows in pattern). *60 (77, 79, 78) sts total; 26 edge sts plus 34 (51, 53, 52) remaining body sts.*

Next row (RS): Work across row 1 of chart D. *2 body sts dec.*

Next row (WS): Work across row 2 of chart D.

7 WRITTEN INSTRUCTIONS

In the following section, for every 8-row repeat of the lace patterns, 6 body stitches are decreased.

Row 1 (RS): K2, ssk, yo, k4, (yo, ssk, k2tog, yo, k1) twice, k3, yo, k2tog, k2, sl1, k2tog (these are body sts), psso. *2 body sts dec.*

Row 2 and all foll WS rows: Sl1, k4, p17, k4.

Row 3: K2, ssk, yo, k1, yo, ssk, k2, yo, sl1, k2tog, psso, yo, k1, yo, k3tog, yo, k2, k2tog, yo, k1, yo, k2tog, k2, ssk (joining edging to 1 body st). *1 body st dec.*

Row 5: K2, ssk, yo, (k2, yo, ssk) twice, k1, (k2tog, yo, k2) twice, yo, k2tog, k2, sl1, k2tog (these are body sts), psso. *2 body sts dec.*

Row 7: K2, ssk, yo, k3, yo, ssk, k2, yo, sl1, k2tog, psso, yo, k2, k2tog, yo, k3, yo, k2tog, k2, ssk (joining edging to 1 body st). *1 body st dec.*

Row 8: Rep row 2.

Rep last 8 rows a further 10 (10, 12, 15) times (88 (88, 104, 128) rows in pattern). *60 (77, 79, 78) sts total; 26 edge sts plus 34 (51, 53, 52) remaining body sts.*

Row 1 (RS): K2, ssk, yo, (k2, k2tog, yo) twice, k1, (yo, ssk, k2) twice, yo, k2tog, k2, sl1, k2tog (these are body sts), psso. *2 body sts dec.*

Row 2 and all foll WS rows: Sl1, k4, p17, k4.

Row 3: K2, ssk, yo, (k1, k2tog, yo, k1) twice, k1, (k1, yo, ssk, k1) twice, yo, k2tog, k2, ssk (joining edging to 1 body st). *1 body st dec.*

Row 5: K2, ssk, yo, k2tog, yo, k2, (k2tog, yo) twice, k1, (yo, ssk) twice, k2, yo, ssk, yo, k2tog, k2, sl1, k2tog (these are body sts), psso. *2 body sts dec.*

Row 7: K2, ssk, yo, k3, (k2tog, yo, k1) twice, (yo, ssk, k1) twice, k2, yo, k2tog, k2, ssk (joining edging to 1 body st). *1 body st dec.*

Row 8: Rep row 2.

Rep last 8 rows a further 4 (7, 7, 7) times (40 (64, 64, 64) rows in pattern). *30 (29, 31, 30) sts total; 26 edge sts plus 4 (3, 5, 4) remaining body sts.*

Rep rows 1 & 2 from step 5 a further 4 (3, 5, 4) times, until all body sts have been decreased. Cast off all lace edge sts and break yarn.

To work the other lace edging, place the 104 (120, 136, 152) live sts from the provisional cast-on edge back on needles (unzipping the crochet edge if required). Then, using working yarn and the cable method, with RS facing, cast on 26 sts as described above and work the lace edge following the same instructions.

Move to step 8.

8 FINISHING

Weave in all ends but do not trim trim, using ends to tidy join between edging and body if needed.

Soak your blanket in lukewarm water and wool wash for 20 minutes. Squeeze out excess water (but do not wring). Press between towels to dry further. Lay your blanket flat to dry, ensuring that the lace edgings are stretched to allow the pattern to really shine. When it is completely dry, trim any remaining ends.

Last 2 rows set chart D pattern. Working next row of chart D each time, continue in pattern as set until chart D has been completed 5 (8, 8, 8) times (40 (64, 64, 64) rows in pattern). *30 (29, 31, 30) sts total; 26 edge sts plus 4 (3, 5, 4) remaining body sts.*

Rep rows 1 & 2 from step 5 a further 4 (3, 5, 4) times, until all body sts have been decreased. *26 edging sts remain.*

Cast off all sts and break yarn.

To work the other lace edging, place the 104 (120, 136, 152) live sts from the provisional cast-on edge back on needles (unzipping the crochet edge if required). Then, using working yarn and the cable method, with RS facing, cast on 26 sts as described in step 5 and work the lace edge following the same instructions.

Move to step 8.

KEY

- ☐ Knit on RS, purl on WS
- ⬛ Purl on RS, knit on WS
- ◣ Ssk
- ◢ K2tog
- ⋌ Sl1, k2tog, psso
- ⋋ K3tog
- ◣ Ssk, joining one edging and one blanket body stitch
- ⋌ Sl1, k2tog, psso, joining one edging and two blanket body stitches
- ○ Yarn over
- ∨ Sl1 purlwise
- ☐ Pattern repeat

CHART D
BLANKET EDGING

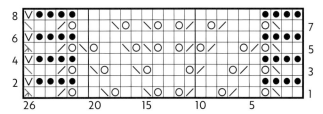

CHART C
BLANKET EDGING

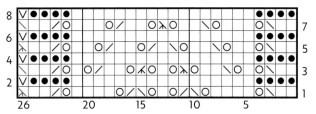

CHART B
BLANKET BODY – MEDIUM AND XL

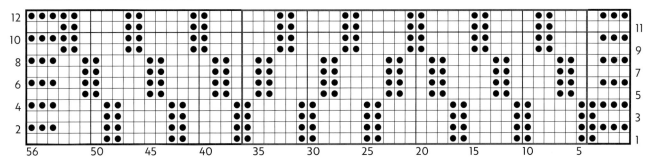

CHART A
BLANKET BODY – SMALL AND LARGE

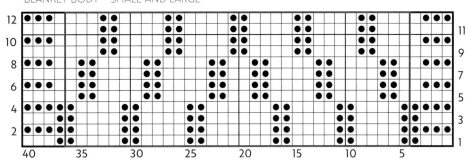

Autumn

TECHNIQUE
GARTER STITCH GRAFTING

Grafting (also known as Kitchener stitch) is a way to join two sets of live stitches invisibly. The first time I grafted the toe of a sock I felt like I had graduated from knitting university. It was so incredibly pleasing that what had been an open set of stitches was now just smooth stocking stitch fabric, with no hint of where the join had taken place. Grafting in stocking stitch has become a fairly familiar technique, thanks at least in part to the enormous popularity of top-down socks. Grafting in garter stitch is arguably easier than in stocking stitch, since the steps on the front and rear needles are the same. However, it's less frequently used, so I almost always refer to a tutorial before I embark on a garter stitch graft.

Martina's Wood Warbler Cowl is knitted on the bias with a provisional cast on. Once you have completed the knitting, you join the cast-on edge to the live stitches with a garter stitch graft (top). This means that the position of the join is only given away if the colours of your stripes at the cast-on edge are different from those of the live stitches (middle).

The key to successful garter stitch grafting is having your two sets of stitches arranged in the correct configuration before you start work. If you look at a piece of garter stitch knitting, you will see that there are garter **ridges** alternating with **valleys** (bottom). Depending on whether you have just worked a right or wrong side row, the garter ridge closest to the needle will either be immediately snug against the needle, or a little further away (with the valley closest to the needle). Looking at the right side of your fabric, if you have just completed the wrong side knit row, the garter ridge will be snug right against the needle. If you have just completed a right side knit row, the ridge will be further from the needle.

VALLEY RIDGE

STEPWISE INSTRUCTIONS FOR GARTER STITCH GRAFTING

i Arrange your needles so that the right side of the fabric is outermost, the cast-on edge is on the front needle, and the live stitches are on your rear needle. You should be able to see that on the front needle the garter ridge is sitting close to the needle.

On the rear needle the garter ridge is sitting further away from the needle. This is easiest to confirm if you look at the wrong side of the fabric on the rear needle. You can then see that the ridge on the wrong side is snug close to the needle. This configuration is called ridge high.

ii Break the yarn attached to your live stitches, leaving a tail long enough to graft. Your pattern will usually tell you how long your tail needs to be. Thread the tail onto a tapestry (blunt) needle.

iii Pass the tapestry needle through the first stitch on the front needle as if to purl. Leave the stitch on the needle.

iv Pass the tapestry needle through the first stitch on the rear needle as if to purl. Leave the stitch on the needle. Steps iii and iv are set-up steps and thus worked once only.

v Pass the tapestry needle through the first stitch on the front needle as if to knit.

vi Slip this stitch off the front needle.

vii Pass the tapestry needle through the next stitch on the front needle as if to purl. Leave the stitch on the needle.

TIP
As you work along the graft, don't tighten your grafted stitches too much. It's much easier to work along at the end, tightening and adjusting the tension to match the surrounding fabric, than it is to loosen the graft if it's too tight.

September

viii Pass the tapestry needle through the first stitch on the rear needle as if to knit.

ix Slip this stitch off the needle.

x Pass the tapestry needle through the next stitch on the rear needle as if to purl. Leave the stitch on the needle.

xi Always keep the grafting yarn below the knitting needle. If necessary, use your tapestry needle to pass it back under the knitting needle.
Repeat steps v–x until you have only 1 stitch remaining on each needle.

Complete the graft as follows:
xii Pass the tapestry needle through the remaining stitch on the front needle as if to knit. Slip this stitch off the needle.

xiii Pass the tapestry needle through the remaining stitch on the rear needle as if to knit. Slip this stitch off the needle.

xiv Once you've completed the graft, have a look and see how much your stitches need to be tightened. You can see here that the line where the two ends were joined is looser than the surrounding fabric.

xv Work along the row, starting at the beginning of the graft, and use your tapestry needle to pull up the slack in adjacent stitches so that the tension matches the surrounding knitting.

Work along the row, stitch by stitch, pulling through the excess yarn.
xvi Once you reach the end of the row, have a look at the knitting and decide whether you need to work along the row again to tighten it further (18).

xvii When you have finished, the grafted row should be almost indistinguishable from the surrounding knitting (19).

REMEMBERING THE GRAFT

I find it helpful to condense the instructions once I have reminded myself of what I'm doing. I use the little phrase "knit, slip, purl". This is the process that you carry out on both front and rear needles – pass the tapestry needle through knitwise (knit), slip the stitch off the needle (slip), then pass the tapestry needle through purlwise (purl) and leave the stitch on the needle. Your yarn needs to pass through each stitch twice before it is complete, so a beginning set up and final section are required for the first and last stitches respectively. The beginning set up section is just the "purl" part worked on the front and then rear needles, and the final section is the "knit, slip" part worked on both needles.

GRAFTING RIDGE LOW GARTER STITCH

If, when you come to work a garter stitch graft, you arrange your knitting with the right side outermost, but your front needle has the garter ridge away from the needle, and the rear needle has the garter ridge snug close to the needle, you are in the ridge low configuration. The simplest way to graft this together is to turn your work inside out. You can then work a ridge high graft with the wrong sides outermost.

GETTING INTERRUPTED

The first few times you graft a set of stitches, it's worth ensuring that you have some peace and quiet and won't be interrupted. It's all too easy to forget what you've just done and lose track of where you are in the instructions. If you do need to pause while grafting, it's a good plan to complete a set of steps v–x before you stop. That will make it easier to pick back up and work out where you are in the process.

STOCKING STITCH GRAFTING

Stocking stitch grafting is worked in a similar manner, but here the front and rear needles are worked differently. Set up your fabric with the right side outermost. You then graft with the phrase "knit, slip, purl, purl, slip, knit". Which means that you work the front needle in the same way as for a garter stitch graft, but on the rear needle you pass the tapestry needle through the first stitch purlwise before slipping it off, then pass the tapestry needle through the next stitch knitwise, leaving it on the needle.

Again, each stitch needs the yarn to pass through it twice, so in order to set up the first stitches you pass the needle purlwise through the first stitch on the front needle, and knitwise through the first stitch on the rear needle. To complete the final stitch on each needle pass the tapestry needle through the stitch on the front needle knitwise, then slip it off, and pass the tapestry needle through the stitch on the rear needle purlwise, then slip it off.

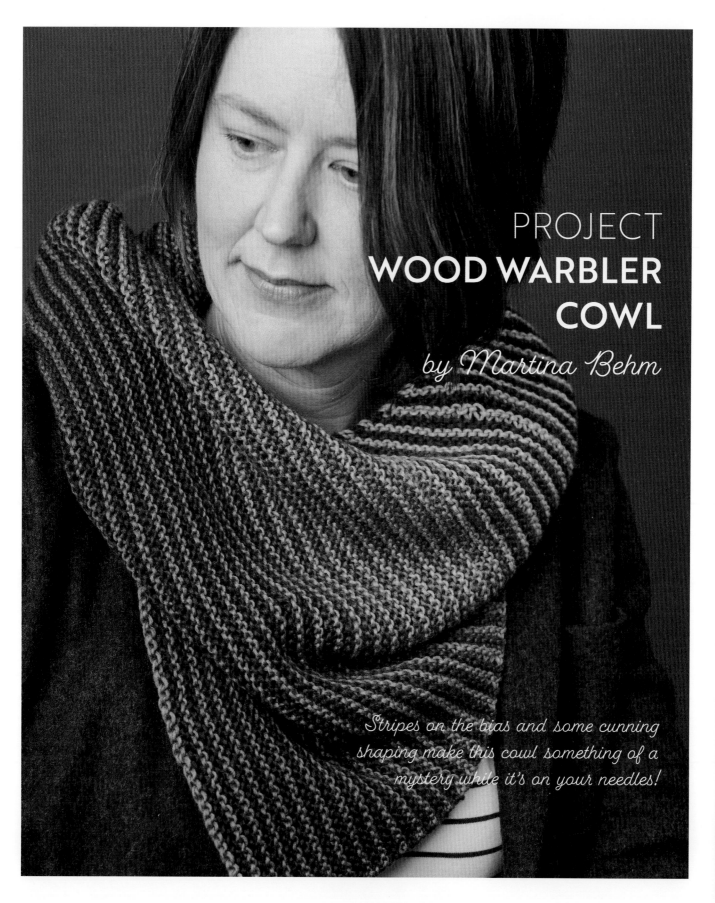

PROJECT
WOOD WARBLER COWL

by Martina Behm

*Stripes on the bias and some cunning
shaping make this cowl something of a
mystery while it's on your needles!*

PROJECT **WOOD WARBLER COWL**

SIZE

Finished circumference: 78cm [30¾in]
Length at deepest point: 46cm [18in]

YARN

Schoppel Wolle Gradient (DK weight; 100% wool; 260m per 100g ball)
Yarn A: Yellow Filter / Gelbfilter (2306); 1 x 100g ball
Yarn B: Shadows / Schatten (1508); 1 x 100g ball

NEEDLES AND NOTIONS

Either 2 sets 5mm [US 8] circular knitting needles, 80cm [32in] long, or size needed to match tension
Or 1 pair 5mm [US 8] interchangeable knitting needle tips and 2 cables plus stoppers
Crochet hook and waste yarn (optional – only required if you're working a crochet provisional cast on instead of Judy's Magic Cast On)

TENSION

18 sts and 36 rows to 10cm [4in] over garter stitch, after washing and blocking

TECHNIQUES

Refer back to August's tutorial (page 52) for instructions on working either the crochet provisional cast on, or Judy's Magic Cast On.

ABBREVIATIONS

A full list of abbreviations appears on the inside back cover.

PATTERN NOTES

The cowl starts with a provisional cast on. Follow the instructions for step 1 if you use Judy's Magic Cast On, or step 2 for a crochet provisional cast on.

The cowl is worked on the bias in garter stitch stripes, and the yarns are carried up the side throughout. You leave the working yarn in the unused colour dangling down on the RS of the piece while you work with the other colour. To keep your edge neat, make sure you are consistent in how you pick up the yarn when you change colours – either pick up the new yarn from under the old, or from above, but stick with whichever you choose. Once the knitting is complete, the cast-on edge is grafted to the end to create the tube shape of the cowl.

PRE-GRAFTING SCHEMATIC

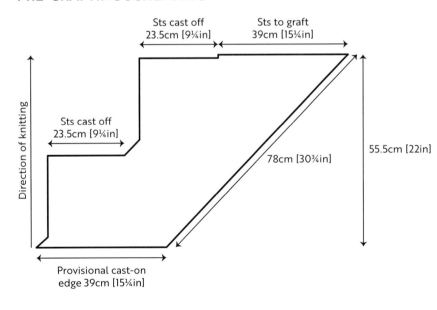

POST-GRAFTING SCHEMATIC

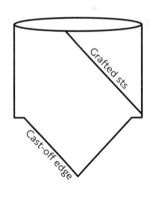

COWL

1 CAST ON WITH JUDY'S MAGIC CAST ON

Move to step 2 for a crochet provisional cast on.

With yarn A, cast on 70 sts using 2 circular needles with Judy's Magic Cast on (you will have 70 sts on each circular needle tip).

Lay the needles in front of you so that the purl bump row is on top, with the needle tips pointing to the right.
Use the rear circular needle to work the pattern. You can remove the needle tips from the cast-on edge, and replace them with stoppers once you have worked a few rows, or you may wish to slip your cast-on sts to waste yarn.
Move to step 3.

2 CAST ON WITH A CROCHET PROVISIONAL CAST ON

Using waste yarn, a crochet hook and a circular needle, cast on 70 sts.
Change to yarn A and knit 2 rows.
Move to step 3.

3 ESTABLISH STRIPES, WORK ON THE BIAS

Row 1 (RS): With yarn B, kfb, knit to last 2 sts, k2tog.
Row 2 (WS): With yarn B, p1, knit to end.
Row 3: With yarn A, kfb, knit to last 2 sts, k2tog.
Row 4: With yarn A, p1, knit to end.
Work rows 1–4 twice more. The stitch count remains constant during this section.

4 WORK INCREASES

Row 1 (RS): With yarn B, kfb, knit to end. *1 st inc.*
Row 2 (WS): With yarn B, p1, knit to end.
Row 3: With yarn A, kfb, knit to end. *1 st inc.*
Row 4: With yarn A, p1, knit to end.
Work rows 1–4 a further 19 times, then work rows 1–3 once more. *42 sts inc; 112 sts.*
Next row (WS): With yarn A, cast off 42 sts, knit to end. *70 sts remain.*

5 WORK ON THE BIAS

Row 1 (RS): With yarn B, kfb, knit to last 2 sts, k2tog.
Row 2 (WS): With yarn B, p1, knit to end.
Row 3: With yarn A, kfb, knit to last 2 sts, k2tog.
Row 4: With yarn A, p1, knit to end.
Work rows 1–4 a further 3 times. The stitch count remains constant during this section.

6 WORK INCREASES

Row 1 (RS): With yarn B, kfb, knit to end. *1 st inc.*
Row 2 (WS): With yarn B, p1, knit to end.
Row 3: With yarn A, kfb, knit to end. *1 st inc.*
Row 4: With yarn A, p1, knit to end.
Work rows 1–4 a further 19 times, then work rows 1–3 once more. *42 sts inc; 112 sts.*
Next row (WS): With yarn A, cast off 42 sts, knit to end. *70 sts remain.*
Break yarn A, leaving a tail to weave in later.
Next row (RS): With yarn B, k70.
Break yarn B, leaving a tail of approx. 2m [2yds] for grafting.

7 GRAFTING

If necessary, unzip the crochet provisional cast-on edge and return the sts to needles. Hold the cowl with the RS outermost, and the cast-on edge in front of the live sts. Following the instructions in the photo tutorial (page 67), work a garter stitch graft to join the remaining 70 sts together with the 70 sts from the cast-on edge, taking care to keep the tension of the graft the same as the surrounding fabric.

8 FINISHING

Weave in all ends but do not trim. Soak your cowl in lukewarm water and wool wash for 20 minutes. Squeeze out excess water (but do not wring). Press between towels to dry further. Lay your cowl flat to dry, paying attention to keep the edges straight. Check that the cowl is folded evenly so that the tips of the cast-off edges match. When the cowl is completely dry, trim any remaining ends.

TECHNIQUE
SHORT-ROW SHAPING IN GARTER STITCH

When you first started knitting, did you ever leave your knitting mid-row, and then work back in the wrong direction when you picked it up again? This is a really common beginner error, and is easily spotted, since it leaves a hole in the middle of the fabric, with one side having a couple of extra rows compared with the other side. What you were actually doing was to unintentionally work a short row.

This is definitely one of those techniques where you can almost imagine early knitters discovering it by accident, and then adapting what started as an error to develop a whole new area of knitting. So many techniques in knitting were developed in different ways at around the same time. It's a lovely combination of happenstance and technical innovation. Short-row shaping is a fantastically powerful way to add three-dimensional shape to your knitted fabric.

Whilst many knitted projects can be worked in flat pieces, with shaping achieved by joining a series of flat shapes, being able to make the fabric itself three-dimensional adds another level of fit to garments and widens the possibilities when creating naturally 3D objects such as toys, or accessories like hats.

CLOSING THE HOLE

You can create short rows by simply stopping mid-row (or round) and turning and working in the opposite direction. However, as you may remember from those early knitting mistakes, this leaves a hole where the row was turned. There are situations where this might be used for decorative effect, but for most applications, the hole is undesirable. There is a wide range of short-row techniques that allow you to use different tricks to close that hole. Indeed, we have already met one of those methods, back in July when we used short rows to turn a heel. When turning a heel, the hole created at the row turn is closed by working a decrease across the gap (ssk or p2tog is used to join the stitch before and the stitch after the gap). Decreasing across the turn of the short row creates a sharp turn in the fabric, as well as causing the original flat knitting to curve around. This is the perfect shape for the back of a heel, but less widely applicable than a method that maintains the original stitch count.

The most well-known method of closing the gap of short rows is the wrap and turn. It is versatile and can be used in a wide range of situations, without changing the number of stitches. It is particularly handy in garter stitch since there is no need to work the wrap with the stitch on following rows. The wraps are disguised by the garter ridges.

Overleaf you will find a set of stepwise instructions for how to add a wrap and turn in garter stitch, as well as instructions for German Short Rows, which are also particularly well suited to garter stitch. Sometimes it's handy to have two options to call on!

October

STEPWISE INSTRUCTIONS FOR WORKING A WRAP AND TURN IN GARTER STITCH

i Work in pattern across your row until you reach the instruction to wrap and turn (w&t). Your yarn is at the back as you've just worked a knit stitch.

ii Slip the next stitch purlwise from left to right needle.

iii Bring your yarn between the needles to the front of the work (as if you were about to purl).

iv Slip the stitch back to the left needle without twisting it. You should be able to see that the slipped stitch now has a wrap at its base.

v Turn, ready to work the next row.

vi Complete the row following your pattern instructions.

WORKING ACROSS THE WRAPPED STITCH

If you have been knitting a series of short rows, it may be many rows before you come to work over the wrapped stitch, or you may cross the wrap on the following row. A series of short rows have been worked in this sample, and you can see the stitches on the right of the needle all have wraps at the base.

If you are working in rib or stocking stitch, then you need to work the wrap with the stitch to hide the turning point, but in garter stitch you can just knit as normal over the wrap, ignoring it completely (8 and 9).

Likewise, when you come to graft the hat together, there is no need to graft the wraps with the stitches, you can just work a garter stitch graft as normal.

STEPWISE INSTRUCTIONS FOR TURNING A GERMAN SHORT ROW IN GARTER STITCH

If your knitting is to be grafted, then working German Short Rows is particularly handy, as they graft very easily.

In the German Short Row method, you pull your stitch up and over the needle at the turn point. This tightens up the spot where a hole would otherwise form, and makes it straightforward to work across on the following rows.

i Work in pattern until you reach the instruction to wrap and turn (w&t). The wrap and turn stitch is going to be your German Short Row stitch. Your yarn is at the back as you've just worked a knit stitch.

ii Knit the next stitch (this is the stitch that would be wrapped in the w&t method).

iii Turn your work ready for the next row (leaving the remaining stitches on the previous row unworked).

iv Slip the first stitch on your left needle (the German Short Row stitch) purlwise to the right needle (with the yarn at the front).

v Pull your working yarn firmly up and over the right needle.

vi The stitch below is stretched up and over the needle and now appears as a "double stitch". The yarn is now on the correct side of the work, ready to knit the next stitch.

vii Keep pulling the working yarn firmly as you knit the next stitch.

viii Work in pattern as directed to the end of the row (or the next turning point). You can see that each of the short-row stitches appears as a double stitch with two legs.

WORKING OVER GERMAN SHORT ROW STITCHES

When you come to work back over the double stitches, you work the double stitch as one.

i Work in pattern until you reach the first double stitch.

ii Insert your right needle into both legs of the double stitch.

iii Knit them together as one.

iv Repeat this process on each double stitch. You will notice that the double stitches are almost invisible from the side that they were knitted, and on the

other side of the fabric, they are hard to spot, but the double stitches can be seen – they appear as a ridge with a doubled stitch, a bit like a p2tog.

GRAFTING GERMAN SHORT ROW STITCHES

The basic instructions for grafting in garter stitch are included in September's tutorial (page 66). Grafting German Short Row stitches is very straightforward – you simply treat each double stitch as if it were a normal stitch.

i Once you've completed the set up section, pass the needle through the first stitch (or double stitch) on the front knitting needle as if to knit.

ii Then slip it off the needle as normal.

iii Pass the needle through the next stitch (or double stitch) on the front needle as if to purl and leave it on the needle. Repeat the same process on the rear needle.

FURTHER APPLICATIONS FOR GARTER STITCH SHORT ROWS

While we usually think of short rows as adding three-dimensionality to knitted fabric, such as in the crown of Woolly Wormhead's Ruschia Hat, or in a garter stitch short row heel in a sock, they can also be used very cleverly in flat fabric. When you combine sets of short rows in a way that's balanced out across all of the fabric (so that all areas have the same total number of rows worked), they can add direction and unusual visual shapes to flat accessories. Particularly in combination with stripes, or colour blocks, short rows can be used to introduce colour in a way that mimics intarsia, without having to juggle multiple balls of yarn in a row.

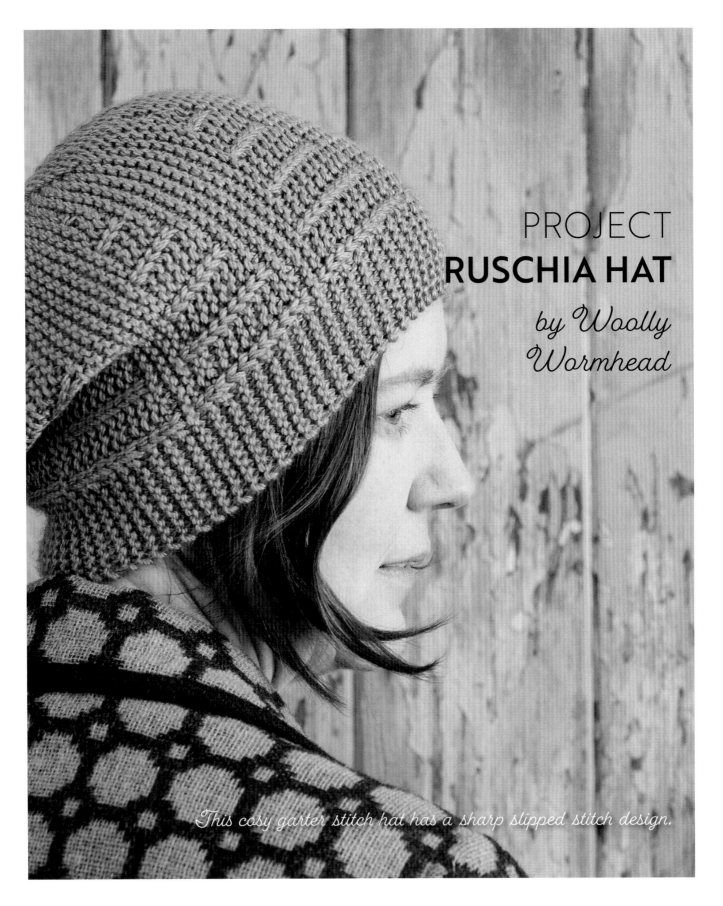

PROJECT
RUSCHIA HAT

by Woolly Wormhead

This cosy garter stitch hat has a sharp slipped stitch design.

SIZES

To fit head circumference: 48.5 (53.5, 58.5) cm [19 (21, 23) in]
Finished hat circumference at brim: 39.5 (45, 50.5) cm [15½ (17¾, 20) in]
Length from crown to brim: 23.5 (25, 26.5) cm [9¼ (9¾, 10½) in]

YARN

Fyberspates Scrumptious Aran (aran weight; 55% merino, 45% silk; 165m per 100g skein)
Water (403) or Slate (405); 1 (1, 2) x 100g skeins

NEEDLES AND NOTIONS

1 pair 4.5mm [US 7] straight needles or size needed to match tension
Similar sized crochet hook
Approx. 2m [2yds] waste yarn
Stitch marker as necessary
Tapestry needle

TENSION

18 sts and 24 rows to 10cm [4in] over stocking stitch using 4.5mm needles
18 sts and 32 rows to 10cm [4in] over garter stitch using 4.5mm needles

TECHNIQUES

Refer back to August's tutorial (page 52) for instructions on working the crochet provisional cast on, and to September's tutorial (page 67) for how to graft in garter stitch.

ABBREVIATIONS

A full list of abbreviations appears on the inside back cover.

PATTERN NOTES

Row tension determines how well the hat fits.
This hat can be knitted using either the wrap and turn method (in which case the wraps do not need to be picked up when you work across them, since they are well hidden in garter stitch), or using the German Short Row method. Both are described in full in the photo tutorial (page 73).
This pattern consists of a series of panels, knitted sideways consecutively. The width of each panel at the brim is 5.5cm [2¼in].
As well as shaping the crown, short rows are also used at the brim to ensure a snug fit.

CHART NOTES

Odd-numbered, right side rows are read from right to left.
Even-numbered, wrong side rows are read from left to right.

HAT

1 CAST ON
Using waste yarn and the crochet provisional cast-on method, cast on 42 (45, 48) sts. Move to step 2 for charted instructions, or step 3 for written instructions.

2 PANEL – CHARTED INSTRUCTIONS
Change to main yarn and work panel as follows:
Row 1 (RS): Work across row 1 of chart, repeating each marked section 1 (2, 3) times in total.
Row 2 (WS): Work across row 2 of chart, repeating each marked section 1 (2, 3) times in total.
Last 2 rows set chart pattern. Working next row of chart each time, continue in pattern as set until chart row 23 has been completed 7 (8, 9) times. (167 (191, 215) rows in pattern). The final row 24 will be replaced by the garter stitch graft.
Move to step 4.

3 PANEL – WRITTEN INSTRUCTIONS
Change to main yarn and work panel as follows:
Row 1 (RS): Knit to end.
Row 2 (WS): K9 (10, 11), sl1 wyif, k31 (33, 35), w&t.
Row 3: Knit to end.
Row 4: K9 (10, 11), sl1 wyif, k3, sl1 wyif, k26 (28, 30), w&t.
Row 5: K31 (33, 35), w&t.
Row 6: Sl1 wyif, (k3, sl1 wyif) twice, k21 (23, 25), w&t.
Row 7: Knit to end.
Row 8: K9 (10, 11), sl1 wyif, (k3, sl1 wyif) 3 times, k16 (18, 20), w&t.
Row 9: Knit to end.
Row 10: K9 (10, 11), sl1 wyif, (k3, sl1 wyif) 4 times, k11 (13, 15), w&t.
Row 11: Knit to end.
Row 12: K9 (10, 11), sl1 wyif, (k3, sl1 wyif) 5 times, k6 (8, 10), w&t.

Row 13: K27 (29, 31), w&t.
Row 14: Sl1 wyif, (k3, sl1 wyif) 4 times, k9 (11, 13), w&t.
Row 15: Knit to end.
Row 16: K9 (10, 11), sl1 wyif, (k3, sl1 wyif) 3 times, k12 (14, 16), w&t.
Row 17: Knit to end.
Row 18: K9 (10, 11), sl1 wyif, (k3, sl1 wyif) twice, k15 (17, 19), w&t.
Row 19: Knit to end.
Row 20: K9 (10, 11), sl1 wyif, k3, sl1 wyif, k18 (20, 22), w&t.
Row 21: K23 (25, 27), w&t.
Row 22: Sl1 wyif, k21 (23, 25), w&t.
Row 23: Knit to end.
Row 24: Knit all sts, working the double stitches as one if you used German Short Rows, and ignoring the wraps if you used the w&t method.
Rep these 24 rows a further 6 (7, 8) times (7 (8, 9) panels worked in total). On the final rep, omit row 24 as this will be replaced by the garter stitch graft.

4 FINISHING
Carefully remove the waste yarn from the provisional cast-on edge stitch by stitch, transferring live stitches to a second needle. You'll graft with the working yarn; cut the working yarn, leaving a 1m [1yd] tail.
When grafting across short rows, you will treat the short rows in exactly the same way as you have throughout the pattern. If you used the wrap and turn method, you can ignore the wraps when grafting, and if you used German Short Rows, pass the tapestry needle through each double stitch as if it were a single stitch.
You will be grafting from the bottom of the hat towards the crown. Once the graft is complete, thread the yarn through the edge stitches and pull to tighten and close the crown. Weave in all ends. Blocking isn't generally necessary.

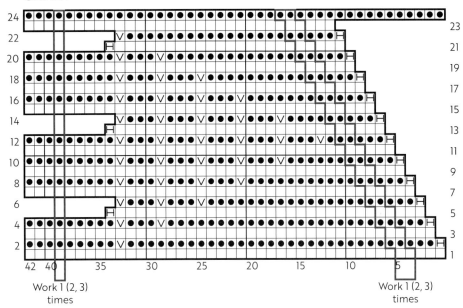

KEY

☐ Knit on RS
▣ Knit on WS
☑ Sl1 wyif on WS
Ⓗ W&t or work German Short Row
☐ Pattern repeat

CHART

Work 1 (2, 3) times

Work 1 (2, 3) times

TECHNIQUE
CHARTED CABLE SYMBOLS

A cable is created when you knit across stitches in the "wrong" order. By changing the order in which stitches are worked, you can create twists in the fabric. Series of cables can be worked over a number of rows, enabling complex rope- and knot-like patterns to be created. Many knitters will knit with confidence from a colourwork chart, but find cable (and lace) charts more challenging; this tutorial will build your confidence in understanding cable symbols used in charts. A greater understanding of how the symbols translate to your knitting will free you from constantly referring to the abbreviations, and will help your knitting to flow more smoothly.

When I was training to teach, there was a great deal of interest in Howard Gardner's *Theory of Multiple Intelligences*, and how understanding different people's preferred learning styles could help us make the curriculum accessible to all. In the same vein, I'm very conscious that some knitters click really well with the visual representation of knitting in charts, and others find them far harder to follow, preferring instead to work from written instructions. Whenever possible, we include written instructions to accompany the charts in our patterns, however there are sometimes situations in which it just isn't practical to provide both charts and written instructions. In these situations patterns are often presented in only charted form. So if knitting from a cable chart is not your first choice of pattern instruction, this tutorial will assist you if you find yourself without the choice.

CABLING WITH OR WITHOUT A CABLE NEEDLE?
My aim here isn't to teach you to cable without a cable needle. Rather it is to explain how to take cable symbols and decipher them directly for your preferred method of cabling (with or without a cable needle). There are many great tutorials out there for how to cable without a cable needle if you'd like to learn this method (see the Extra Resources section, page 115).

A YEAR OF **TECHNIQUES**

FIGURE 1

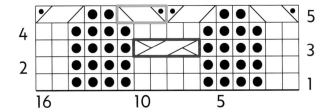

FIGURE 2

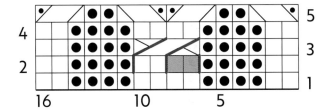

FIGURE 3

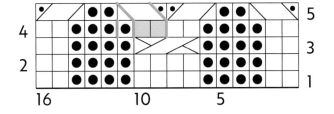

READING SYMBOLS AND USING A CABLE NEEDLE

HOW MANY STITCHES ARE INVOLVED IN THE CABLE?
When working out how a cable is knitted, the first job is to understand how many stitches are involved. When you are knitting cables from a chart, you need to count how many stitches the cable symbol covers. The cable outlined in pink in figure 1 covers 4 stitches, and the cable outlined in blue covers just 3.

HOW MANY STITCHES GO ON MY CABLE NEEDLE?
To work this out, you need to look at how the stitches are divided in the cable symbol. Imagine that the diagonal line, that ends in the middle of the bottom of the cable symbol, is extended below the cable, as shown in figure 2. Looking at the section below the cable symbol, on the right hand side (filled in pink), shows us how many stitches to slip to the cable needle. In figure 2 we are slipping the first 2 stitches to a cable needle. In figure 3 (filled in blue), it is also 2 stitches being slipped to a cable needle.

AND DOES THE CABLE NEEDLE NEED TO BE AT THE FRONT, OR AT THE BACK?
When a cable leans to the left, the cable needle is held at the front, and when a cable leans to the right, the cable needle is held at the rear. So for the cable in figure 2, the cable needle needs to be held at the back. Can you visualise the 2 stitches (filled in pink) passing behind the next 2 stitches? And for the cable in figure 3, the cable leans to the left, so you need to hold the cable needle at the front of the work.

HOW MANY STITCHES DO I WORK OFF THE LEFT NEEDLE?
You know the total number of stitches involved in the cable, and you've worked out how many stitches you need to put on your cable needle, so the remainder are worked off the left needle. You can visualise these on the charted symbol as the group of stitches on the left, below the symbol. The cable in figure 2 has 2 stitches worked off the left needle, and the cable in figure 3 has 1 stitch worked.

DO I KNIT OR PURL?
Now that you have the correct number of stitches on your cable needle, and you know how many stitches you are working off the left needle, you just need to work out whether they are knitted, purled, or worked some other way. To do this you look across the cable symbol itself. In figure 2 the cable doesn't have any extra symbols in it – it is just empty diagonal lines. This tells us that all of the stitches in the cable are knitted. So you knit 2 stitches from the left needle, and then you knit 2 stitches from the cable needle. In figure 3, there is a purl dot in the first stitch space on the right of the cable symbol, so you purl the first stitch from the left needle. Then the diagonal strip passing at the front of the cable doesn't have any other symbols on it, so it's knitted. This means that you then knit the 2 stitches on the cable needle.

November

WORKED EXAMPLES

2/2 RC

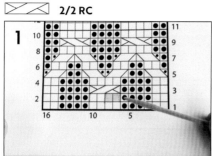

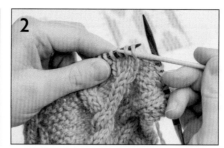

The cable symbol covers 4 stitches. If we imagine lines down from the bottom of the diagonal strips, we can

see that it divides into two sets of 2 stitches. 2 stitches are therefore slipped to the cable needle, which is held at the

back, because the cable leans to the right. Since there are no other symbols on the cable, all of the stitches are

knitted. So knit 2 stitches (4 stitches total minus 2 stitches on the cable needle) from the left needle,

then knit the 2 stitches from the cable needle.

You should be able to see that 2 knit stitches have crossed 2 knit stitches, leaning to the right.

2/1 LPC

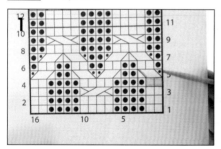

The cable symbol covers 3 stitches. Imagine lines down from the bottom of the diagonal strip – we can see that

it divides into 2 stitches on the right and 1 stitch on the left. 2 stitches are therefore slipped to the cable needle.

The cable needle is held at the front, because the cable leans to the left. The first symbol in the cable (1) is a purl dot, so 1 stitch (3 stitches total minus 2

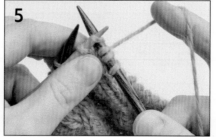

stitches on the cable needle) is purled from the left needle (3 and 4).

There are no other symbols on the diagonal strip, so the stitches from the cable needle are knitted.

You can see that 2 knit stitches have crossed 1 purl stitch, leaning to the left.

2/1 RPC

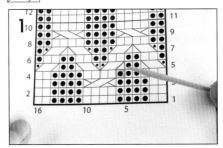

The cable symbol covers 3 stitches. Imagine lines down from the bottom of the diagonal strip – we can see that

it divides into 1 stitch on the right and 2 stitches on the left. 1 stitch is therefore slipped to the cable needle. The cable

needle is held at the back because the cable leans to the right. There are 2 stitches to be worked off the left needle

(3 stitches total minus 1 stitch on the cable needle), and the cable symbol has no extra symbols in the diagonal strip, so these stitches are knitted. Looking across

the cable symbol, the final stitch has a purl dot in it, so you purl the stitch from the cable needle. You should be able to see that 2 knit stitches have crossed 1 purl

stitch, leaning to the right.
You can practise working out cables by looking at the chart symbols and then comparing them with the instructions in the abbreviations.

FIGURE 4

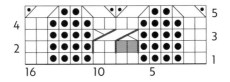

FIGURE 5

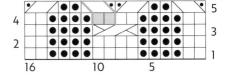

CABLING WITHOUT A CABLE NEEDLE

One of the best ways to speed up your cabling is to learn to cable without a cable needle. It also makes it much easier to cable on the move, since you don't have a cable needle to drop down the back of a car seat, or lose on the bus. Here are stepwise instructions for working out how to work a cable symbol without a cable needle.

HOW MANY STITCHES ARE INVOLVED IN THE CABLE?
This is worked the same way as for cabling with a cable needle (page 81).

HOW ARE THE STITCHES DIVIDED?
To work this out, you need to look at how the stitches are divided in the cable symbol. Imagine that the lines on the diagonal part of the cable symbol are extended below the cable, as shown in figure 4. Looking at the section below the cable symbol, the left hand side (the stitches not coloured in), shows us how many stitches to pick up with the right needle tip. In figure 4 we skip the first 2 stitches (the coloured in ones) and we pick up 2 stitches on the right needle (the uncoloured stitches). In figure 5, we skip the first 2 stitches on the left needle (the stitches coloured in blue) and just 1 stitch is being picked up on the right needle (the uncoloured stitch).

AND DO I PICK UP THE STITCHES FROM THE FRONT OR THE BACK?
If the cable leans to the left, you need to pick up the stitch(es) at the back of the work. If the cable leans to the right, you need to pick up the stitch(es) from the front of the work. Once you have picked up the left hand group of stitches on your right needle tip, carefully pull your left needle out of all the stitches involved in the cable. The left hand group of stitches will be on your right needle, and the right hand group of stitches will be off the needle tip. Pick up these stitches with your left needle tip, then return the slipped stitches on your right needle to the left needle.

November

DO I KNIT OR PURL?

Now that you have the stitches in the correct order on your right needle, you just need to work out whether they are knitted, purled, or worked some other way. To do this you look across the cable symbol itself. In figure 4 the cable doesn't have any extra symbols in it – it is just empty diagonal lines. This tells us that all of the stitches in the cable are knitted. So you knit all 4 stitches. In figure 5, there is a purl dot in the first stitch space on the right of the cable symbol, so you purl the first stitch from the left needle. Then the diagonal strip passing at the front of the cable doesn't have any other symbols on it, so it's knitted. This means that you then knit the next 2 stitches.

WORKED EXAMPLES

2/2 RC

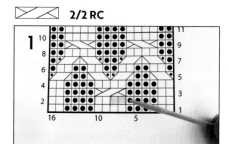

The cable symbol covers 4 stitches. If we imagine lines down from the bottom of the diagonal strips, we can see that it divides into two sets of 2 stitches. There are 2 stitches in the group on the left of the cable, and the cable leans to the right, so you skip 2 stitches (the coloured in right hand group) and pick up 2 stitches with your right needle tip at the front of the work.

Slide the left needle out of all 4 stitches involved in the cable. You have 2 stitches on the right needle and 2 stitches hanging in mid-air.

Use the left needle tip to pick up the hanging stitches. Return the slipped stitches on the right needle to the left needle.

You can now see that you have changed the order of the stitches on the right needle. Work across the stitches following the symbols on the cable symbol.

In this case there are no extra symbols so all 4 stitches are knitted. You should be able to see that 2 knit stitches have crossed 2 knit stitches, leaning to the right.

2/1 LPC

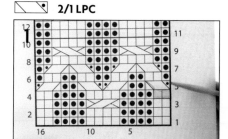

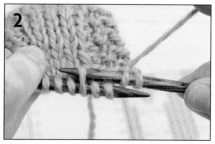

The cable symbol covers 3 stitches. Imagining a line down from the diagonal, it divides into 2 stitches on the right and 1 stitch on the left.

You skip the first 2 stitches (the right hand group below the symbol), and pick up 1 stitch from behind with your right needle tip (as the cable leans to the left).

Carefully slide the left needle out of all 3 stitches involved in the cable. You have 1 stitch on your right needle and 2 stitches hanging in mid-air.

Use your left needle tip to pick up the hanging stitches. Return the slipped stitches on the right needle to the left needle. You have changed the order of

stitches on the needle. Work across them following the symbols on the cable – the first symbol is a small purl dot, so you purl the first stitch on the left needle. There

are no further symbols on the cable, the diagonal strip is empty, so the remaining 2 stitches are knitted. You should be able to see that 2 knit stitches have crossed 1 purl stitch, leaning to the left.

2/1 RPC

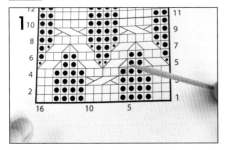

The cable symbol covers 3 stitches. Imagine lines down from the bottom of the diagonal strip – we can see that it divides into 1 stitch on the right and 2 stitches on the left. You skip the first stitch

(the right hand group below the symbol), and pick up 2 stitches from the front with your right needle tip (as the cable leans to the right). Carefully slide the left needle out of all 3 stitches involved in the cable.

You have 2 stitches on your right needle and 1 stitch hanging in mid-air. Use your left needle tip to pick up the hanging stitch. Return the slipped stitches from the right to the left needle. You have changed

the order of stitches on the needle. Work across the stitches following the symbols on the cable symbol – the first 2 stitches

(on the diagonal) are blank so they are knitted, and the 3rd stitch has a purl dot, so it is purled.

You should be able to see that 2 knit stitches have crossed 1 purl stitch, leaning to the right.

PRACTISE!
The best way to speed up your cabling from charts is to practise. It may seem slow and laborious at first to follow the stepwise instructions, but over time it will get quicker. And next time you're confronted with an unfamiliar chart symbol, you can at least make a start at understanding what you should be doing. Comparing the symbol with the abbreviations will confirm whether you've correctly deciphered the code.

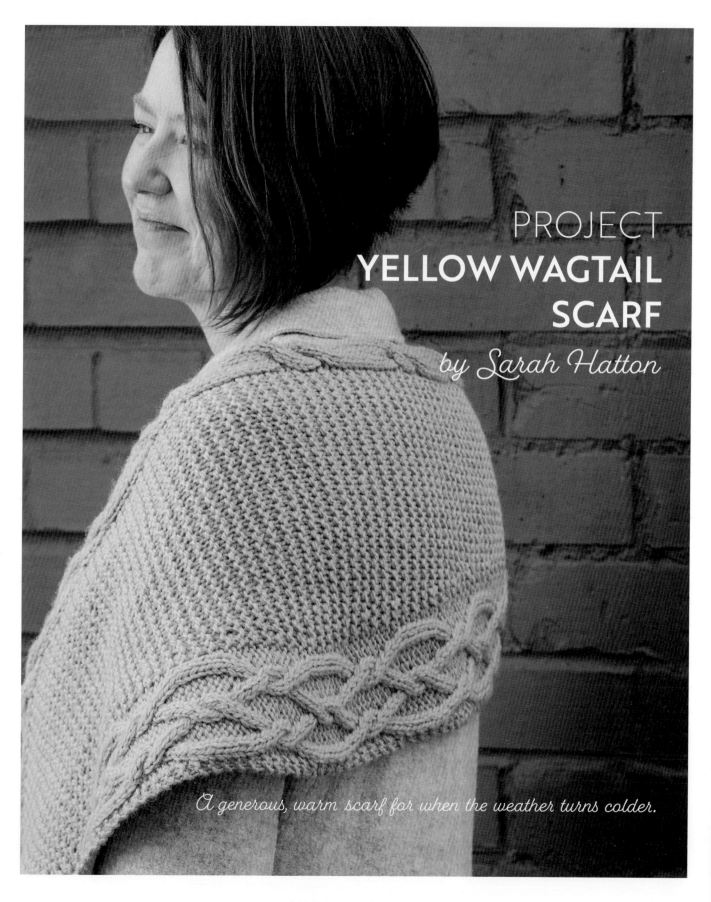

PROJECT
YELLOW WAGTAIL SCARF
by Sarah Hatton

A generous, warm scarf for when the weather turns colder.

PROJECT **YELLOW WAGTAIL SCARF**

SIZE
Width: 18.5cm [7¼in] at narrowest and 38.5cm [15in] at widest
Length: 214cm [84¼in]

YARN
Jamieson & Smith Shetland Aran Worsted (aran weight; 100% Shetland wool; 61m per 50g ball)
Auld Gold; 7 x 50g balls

NEEDLES AND NOTIONS
1 pair 5.5mm [US 9] knitting needles, or size needed to match tension
Cable needle (unless working the cabling without a cable needle technique)
Stitch markers

TENSION
14 sts and 26 rows to 10cm [4in] over garter stitch using 5.5mm needles, **before** washing and blocking
12 sts and 18 rows to 10cm [4in] over garter stitch using 5.5mm needles, **after** washing and blocking
Cable panel A of 6 sts measures 3.5cm [1½in] wide, after washing and blocking
Cable panel B of 16 sts measures 9cm [3½in] wide, after washing and blocking

ABBREVIATIONS
2/1 RPC   slip next stitch to cable needle and hold at back, k2 then p1 from cable needle
2/1 LPC   slip next 2 stitches to cable needle and hold at front, p1 then k2 from cable needle
2/2 RC   slip next 2 stitches to cable needle and hold at back, k2 then k2 from cable needle
2/2 LC   slip next 2 stitches to cable needle and hold at front, k2 then k2 from cable needle
3/3 RC   slip next 3 stitches to cable needle and hold at back, k3 then k3 from cable needle

A full list of abbreviations appears on the inside back cover.

PATTERN NOTES
This pattern is provided in both charted and written formats. This month's technique is to practise reading charted cable symbols, but many knitters find it helpful to start work from written instructions and then move to the chart once they have the pattern established. You can mix and match between the two formats as you please.
The pattern is essentially two cable borders, with a garter stitch centre. Shaping is worked in the garter stitch section to create an asymmetric shape, thus keeping your neck warm, but with less fabric where the scarf hangs.

CHART NOTES
Odd-numbered, right side rows are read from right to left.
Even-numbered wrong side rows are read from left to right.

November

SCARF

1 CAST ON AND INCREASE

Cast on 26 sts (the thumb or long-tail methods will give the neatest finish).

Set-up row 1 (RS): Purl.

Set-up row 2 (WS): K3, M1L, k12, M1L, k5, M1L, k6. *3 sts inc; 29 sts.*

Move to step 2 for charted instructions, or step 3 for written instructions.

2 SCARF BODY – CHARTED INSTRUCTIONS

Row 1 (RS): K2, work 16 sts across row 1 of chart A, p1, pm, knit to last 7 sts, p1, work 6 sts across row 1 of chart B.

Row 2 (WS): Work 6 sts across row 2 of chart B, knit to marker, slm, k1, work 16 sts across row 2 of chart A, k2.

These 2 rows set charts A and B. Work a further 2 rows as set, ending with RS facing for next row.

Row 5 (RS): K2, work 16 sts across row 5 of chart A, p1, slm, k1, M1R, knit to last 7 sts, p1, work 6 sts across row 5 of chart B. *1 st inc.*

This row sets the increases (k1, M1R after the marker). Working increases as set on chart rows 5, 11 and 17, each time you reach them, continue until chart row 4 has been completed for the 9th time (a total of 164 chart rows worked). *24 sts inc; 53 sts.*

Row 165 (RS): K2, work 16 sts across row 5 of chart A, p1, slm, k1, sl1, k1, psso, knit to last 7 sts, p1, work 6 sts across row 5 of chart B. *1 st dec.*

This row sets the decreases (k1, sl1, k1, psso after the marker). Working decreases as set on chart rows 5, 11 and 17, each time you reach them, continue until chart row 20 has been completed for the 10th time (a total of 200 chart rows worked). *6 sts dec; 47 sts remain.*

Now working decreases as set on chart rows 5 and 15 only, continue until chart row 20 has been completed for the 19th time (a total of 380 chart rows worked). *18 sts dec; 29 sts remain.*

Work row 1 as set on charts.

Move to step 4.

3 SCARF BODY – WRITTEN INSTRUCTIONS

Row 1 (RS): (K4, p4) twice, k2, p1, pm, knit to last 7 sts, p1, k6.

Row 2 (WS): K1, p5, knit to marker, slm, k1, p2, k4, p4, k4, p2, k2.

Row 3: K4, p4, 2/2 RC, p4, k2, p1, slm, knit to last 7 sts, p1, k6.

Row 4: K1, p5, knit to marker, slm, k1, p2, k4, p4, k4, p2, k2.

Row 5 (inc): K2, (2/1 LPC, p2, 2/1 RPC) twice, p1, slm, k1, M1R, knit to last 7 sts, p1, k6. *1 st inc.*

Row 6: K1, p5, knit to marker, slm, (k2, p2) 4 times, k3.

Row 7: K2, (p1, 2/1 LPC, 2/1 RPC, p1) twice, p1, slm, knit to last 7 sts, p1, 3/3 RC.

Row 8: K1, p5, knit to marker, slm, k3, (p4, k4) twice.

Row 9: K2, (p2, 2/2 LC, p2) twice, p1, slm, knit to last 7 sts, p1, k6.

Row 10: K1, p5, knit to marker, slm, k3, (p4, k4) twice.

Row 11 (inc): K2, p2, k4, p4, k4, p3, slm, k1, M1R, knit to last 7 sts, p1, k6. *1 st inc.*

Row 12: K1, p5, knit to marker, slm, k3, (p4, k4) twice.

Row 13: K2, (p2, 2/2 LC, p2) twice, p1, slm, knit to last 7 sts, p1, 3/3 RC.

Row 14: K1, p5, knit to marker, slm, k3, (p4, k4) twice.

Row 15: K2, (p1, 2/1 RPC, 2/1 LPC, p1) twice, p1, slm, knit to last 7 sts, p1, k6.

Row 16: K1, p5, knit to marker, slm, (k2, p2) 4 times, k3.

Row 17 (inc): K2, (2/1 RPC, p2, 2/1 LPC) twice, p1, slm, k1, M1R, knit to last 7 sts, p1, k6. *1 st inc.*

Row 18: K1, p5, knit to marker, slm, k1, p2, k4, p4, k4, p2, k2.

Row 19: K4, p4, 2/2 RC, p4, k2, p1, slm, knit to last 7 sts, p1, k6.

Row 20: K1, p5, knit to marker, slm, k1, p2, k4, p4, k4, p2, k2.

Rep last 20 rows a further 7 times (a total of 160 pattern rows worked). *24 sts inc; 53 sts.*

Row 161 (RS): (K4, p4) twice, k2, p1, slm, knit to last 7 sts, p1, k6.

Row 162 (WS): K1, p5, knit to marker, slm, k1, p2, k4, p4, k4, p2, k2.

Row 163: K4, p4, 2/2 RC, p4, k2, p1, slm, knit to last 7 sts, p1, k6.

Row 164: K1, p5, knit to marker, slm, k1, p2, k4, p4, k4, p2, k2.

Row 165 (dec): K2, (2/1 LPC, p2, 2/1 RPC) twice, p1, slm, k1, sl1, k1, psso, knit to last 7 sts, p1, k6. *1 st dec.*

Row 166: K1, p5, knit to marker, slm, (k2, p2) 4 times, k3.

Row 167: K2, (p1, 2/1 LPC, 2/1 RPC, p1) twice, p1, slm, knit to last 7 sts, p1, 3/3 RC.
Row 168: K1, p5, knit to marker, slm, k3, (p4, k4) twice.
Row 169: K2, (p2, 2/2 LC, p2) twice, p1, slm, knit to last 7 sts, p1, k6.
Row 170: K1, p5, knit to marker, slm, k3, (p4, k4) twice.
Row 171 (dec): K2, p2, k4, p4, k4, p3, slm, k1, sl1, k1, psso, knit to last 7 sts, p1, k6. *1 st dec.*
Row 172: K1, p5, knit to marker, slm, k3, (p4, k4) twice.
Row 173: K2, (p2, 2/2 LC, p2) twice, p1, slm, knit to last 7 sts, p1, 3/3 RC.
Row 174: K1, p5, knit to marker, slm, k3, (p4, k4) twice.
Row 175: K2, (p1, 2/1 RPC, 2/1 LPC, p1) twice, p1, slm, knit to last 7 sts, p1, k6.
Row 176: K1, p5, knit to marker, slm, (k2, p2) 4 times, k3.
Row 177 (dec): K2, (2/1 RPC, p2, 2/1 LPC) twice, p1, slm, k1, sl1, k1, psso, knit to last 7 sts, p1, k6. *1 st dec.*
Row 178: K1, p5, knit to marker, slm, k1, p2, k4, p4, k4, p2, k2.
Row 179: K4, p4, 2/2 RC, p4, k2, p1, slm, knit to last 7 sts, p1, k6.
Row 180: K1, p5, knit to marker, slm, k1, p2, k4, p4, k4, p2, k2.
Rep last 20 rows once more (a total of 200 pattern rows worked). *6 sts dec; 47 sts remain.*

Row 201 (RS): (K4, p4), k2, p1, slm, knit to last 7 sts, p1, k6.
Row 202 (WS): K1, p5, knit to marker, slm, k1, p2, k4, p4, k4, p2, k2.
Row 203: K4, p4, 2/2 RC, p4, k2, p1, slm, knit to last 7 sts, p1, k6.
Row 204: K1, p5, knit to marker, slm, k1, p2, k4, p4, k4, p2, k2.
Row 205 (dec): K2, (2/1 LPC, p2, 2/1 RPC) twice, p1, slm, k1, sl1, k1, psso, knit to last 7 sts, p1, k6. *1 st dec.*
Row 206: K1, p5, knit to marker, slm, (k2, p2) 4 times, k3.
Row 207: K2, (p1, 2/1 LPC, 2/1 RPC, p1) twice, p1, slm, knit to last 7 sts, p1, 3/3 RC.
Row 208: K1, p5, knit to marker, slm, k3, (p4, k4) twice.
Row 209: K2, (p2, 2/2 LC, p2) twice, p1, slm, knit to last 7 sts, p1, k6.
Row 210: K1, p5, knit to marker, slm, k3, (p4, k4) twice.
Row 211: K2, p2, k4, p4, k4, p3, slm, knit to last 7 sts, p1, k6.
Row 212: K1, p5, knit to marker, slm, k3, (p4, k4) twice.
Row 213: K2, (p2, 2/2 LC, p2) twice, p1, slm, knit to last 7 sts, p1, 3/3 RC.
Row 214: K1, p5, knit to marker, slm, k3, (p4, k4) twice.
Row 215 (dec): K2, (p1, 2/1 RPC, 2/1 LPC, p1) twice, p1, slm, k1, sl1, k1, psso, knit to last 7 sts, p1, k6. *1 st dec.*
Row 216: K1, p5, knit to marker, slm, (k2, p2) 4 times, k3.
Row 217: K2, (2/1 RPC, p2, 2/1 LPC) twice, p1, slm, knit to last 7 sts, p1, k6.
Row 218: K1, p5, knit to marker, slm, k1, p2, k4, p4, k4, p2, k2.
Row 219: K4, p4, 2/2 RC, p4, k2, p1, slm, knit to last 7 sts, p1, k6.
Row 220: K1, p5, knit to marker, slm, k1, p2, k4, p4, k4, p2, k2.
Rep last 20 rows a further 8 times (a total of 380 pattern rows worked). *18 sts dec; 29 sts remain.*
Rep row 201 once more.
Move to step 4.

4 DECREASES
Row 382 (WS): K3, k2tog, k11, k2tog, k4, k2tog, k5. *3 sts dec; 26 sts.*
Next row (RS): Purl.
Cast off knitwise on WS.

5 FINISHING
Weave in all ends but do not trim.
Soak your scarf in lukewarm water and wool wash for 20 minutes. Squeeze out excess water (but do not wring). Press between towels to dry further. Lay your scarf flat to dry, pinning it to the measurements given. When it is completely dry, trim any remaining ends.

KEY

☐ Knit on RS, purl on WS

▣ Purl on RS, knit on WS

2/1 RPC slip next stitch to cable needle and hold at back, k2 then p1 from cable needle

2/1 LPC slip next 2 stitches to cable needle and hold at front, p1 then k2 from cable needle

2/2 RC slip next 2 stitches to cable needle and hold at back, k2 then k2 from cable needle

2/2 LC slip next 2 stitches to cable needle and hold at front, k2 then k2 from cable needle

3/3 RC slip next 3 stitches to cable needle and hold at back, k3 then k3 from cable needle

CHART B   **CHART A**

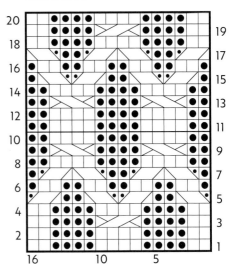

Winter

December

TECHNIQUE **Afterthought Heels (and Thumbs)**
PROJECT **Hedera Helix Socks**
DESIGNER **Jim Arnall-Culliford**

January

TECHNIQUE **Dominance in Fair Isle Knitting**
PROJECT **Shaila Mittens**
DESIGNER **Ella Gordon**

February

TECHNIQUE **Steeks**
PROJECT **Oorik Tank Top**
DESIGNER **Mary Jane Mucklestone**

TECHNIQUE
AFTERTHOUGHT HEELS (& THUMBS)

There are times when you want to keep the flow of your knitting. You don't want to stop and do something different, you just want to keep going. Perhaps you're working with a gradient yarn and you want that beautiful rainbow to continue uninterrupted throughout your project. Or maybe you're in the rhythm of a cable or Fair Isle pattern, and stopping to turn the heel will upset that nice Zen place you're in. Or perhaps you prefer the fit of an afterthought heel or thumb? Whatever your motivation, an afterthought opening in your knitting is a handy trick to call upon.

The principle is simple: decide how many stitches wide you would like your opening in the fabric to be, and then work that many stitches in waste yarn, before knitting over them again in the main yarn and continuing on your way. At the end of the project you can then pick up stitches around the waste yarn, remove it, and knit down from the opening to create your heel, thumb, pocket or whatever else you desire! Regardless of what you are using your afterthought opening for, the process is exactly the same.

I recommend using a smooth mercerised cotton for your waste yarn, as it will be easy to remove later. You can use wool, but it has more of a tendency to felt to the neighbouring stitches, making it harder to unravel. You can omit adding waste yarn stitches entirely, and simply snip the main yarn and unravel it back the required number of stitches in each direction at the end of the project. I have found, though, that using the waste yarn just makes it so much easier to see which stitches to pick up, and so is worth the extra step. It also makes it less likely that you will drop a stitch when you are opening your heel, thumb or pocket.

STEPWISE INSTRUCTIONS FOR ADDING A WASTE YARN OPENING

i Join in your waste yarn. For an afterthought heel, you will likely be working across at least half of the stitches on the back leg / sole side of the round. If you are working on double-pointed needles, it may be worth moving your stitches around so that you can start the waste yarn section at the start of a needle.

ii Knit across the stitches using your waste yarn, as instructed in your pattern.

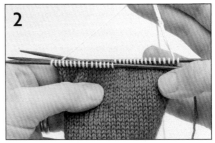

iii When you have worked sufficient stitches, loosely tie the ends of the waste yarn together so that the stitches don't unravel.

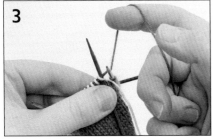

iv If you are working on circular needles you will need to slip the waste yarn stitches back to your left needle. On double-pointed needles, you may be able to slide the stitches back to the other end of the needle. Pick up your main yarn again, ready to work across the waste yarn stitches.

v Work in pattern over the waste yarn stitches, using your main yarn.

vi You will see that you now have a section of waste yarn in your fabric. After completion of the sock (or mitten or garment), you will return to these stitches, unpick the waste yarn and work an afterthought heel (thumb or pocket).

STEPWISE INSTRUCTIONS FOR OPENING AN AFTERTHOUGHT HEEL (THUMB OR POCKET)

i When you have completed the main part of the knitting on your project, return to your waste yarn stitches. Look at the V shape of each of the waste yarn stitches, and identify the row of main yarn stitches below the waste yarn.

ii Using a needle a size or so smaller than the needles you are using for the project, pick up the right leg of each of the main yarn stitches below the row of waste yarn.

iii Continue picking up the right leg of each of the stitches across the row. If you are using double-pointed needles, you may need to use two.

December

iv Turn your work through 180° and work across the other side of the waste yarn in exactly the same way.

v Once all of your stitches are picked up, you can remove the waste yarn, either by undoing the knot and pulling the ends through, or by carefully cutting it out.

vi Continue to remove the waste yarn, making sure all of the stitches are safely on your needles.

vii Once the waste yarn is completely removed, it is worth checking that you have all the stitches on your needles, particularly those at the corners.

viii Now join in your main yarn, and using your correct pattern size needles, work across one side of the waste yarn opening.

ix When you reach what was the end of the waste yarn row of stitches, you will see that there is a gap.

x Pick up and knit a stitch or two in this gap (your pattern will normally tell you how many stitches to pick up).

xi Work across the other side of the waste yarn opening with your main yarn, making sure you are using the correct sized needles.

xii Pick up and knit a stitch or two in the gap at the end of this side too.

xiii You are now ready to knit your heel, thumb or pocket in the round (12).

VARIATIONS ON A THEME
Afterthought openings are a really versatile way to take your knitting in a different direction. If you can imagine your project as a series of joined tubes, any point where the tubes divide you could use an afterthought opening. Knitting a soft toy? Make the head and body as one (shaped) tube, and then use afterthought openings to add arms and maybe legs later. And should you decide later that the opening is in the wrong place, you can always graft the stitches back together, and make a true afterthought opening by cutting the main yarn in a better spot.

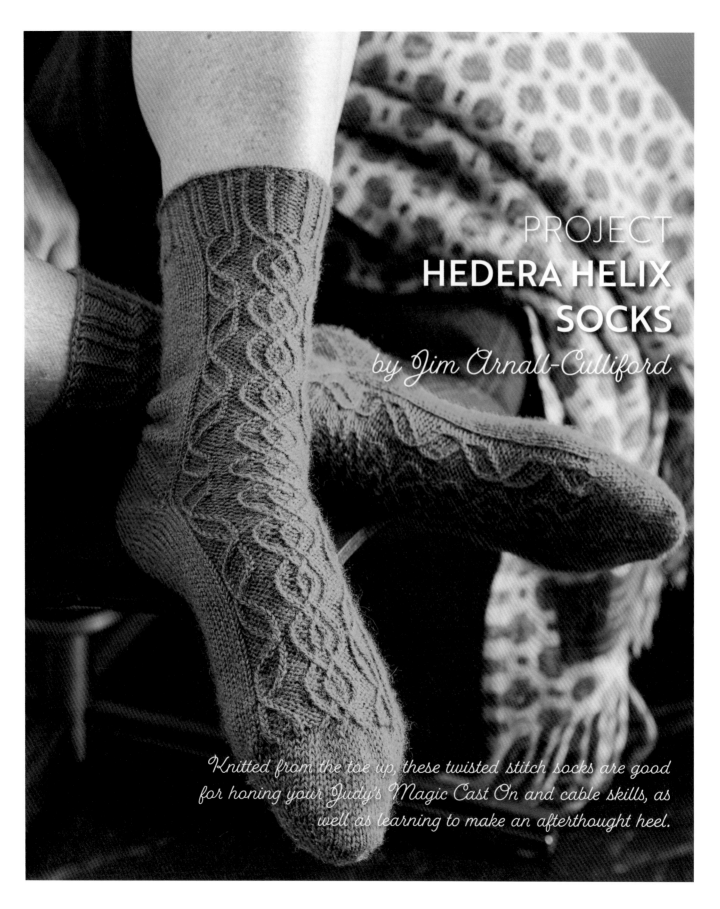

PROJECT
HEDERA HELIX SOCKS
by Jim Arnall-Culliford

Knitted from the toe up, these twisted stitch socks are good for honing your Judy's Magic Cast On and cable skills, as well as learning to make an afterthought heel.

December

SIZES

Small (Medium, Large, XL)
To fit foot circumference: 20.5 (23, 25.5, 28) cm [8 (9, 10, 11) in]
Actual foot circumference of sock (unstretched): 16 (18, 21, 24) cm [6¼ (7, 8¼, 9½) in]
Length of leg to top of heel: 17cm [6¾in]
Foot length is fully adjustable within the pattern. Finished sock measures 0.5cm [¼in] less than actual foot length to ensure a good fit.

YARN

Schoppel Wolle Admiral 6ply (sport weight (between 4ply and DK); 75% wool, 25% polyamide; 400m per 150g ball)
Mars Green / Marsgrün (6601); 1 x 150g ball

NEEDLES AND NOTIONS

2 sets 2.75mm [US 2] circular needles for Judy's Magic Cast On
1 set 2.75mm [US 2] double-pointed needles or your preferred needles for working small circumferences in the round, or size needed to match tension
Stitch marker; Cable needle

TENSION

32 sts and 42 rounds to 10cm [4in] over stocking stitch in the round, after washing and blocking
28 sts of cable panel measures 6.5cm [2½in] unstretched

TECHNIQUES

Refer back to August's tutorial (page 57) for how to work Judy's Magic Cast On for the closed base of a tube.

ABBREVIATIONS

1/1 LT	Slip 1 st to cable needle and hold in front, k1 tbl; k1 tbl from cable needle
1/1 RT	Slip 1 st to cable needle and hold in back, k1 tbl; k1 tbl from cable needle
1/1 LPT	Slip 1 st to cable needle and hold in front, p1; k1 tbl from cable needle
1/1 RPT	Slip 1 st to cable needle and hold in back, k1 tbl; p1 from cable needle

A full list of abbreviations appears on the inside back cover.

PATTERN NOTES

These socks are cast on at the toe using Judy's Magic Cast On, before increases are worked to reach the required foot circumference. The foot is then worked with a twisted stitch pattern on the instep and stocking stitch on the sole, before adding a section of waste yarn stitches for the heel. The leg is then worked in the same way as the foot, before a rib cuff is knitted and the stitches are cast off using a stretchy method. The pattern instructions are provided in both charted and written formats, allowing you to practise reading charted cable symbols if you desire.

CHART NOTES

Read all chart rows from right to left.

SOCK
MAKE TWO ALIKE

1 TOE

Cast on 18 (20, 22, 24) sts using Judy's Magic Cast On (9 (10, 11, 12) sts on each needle tip).
Knit 1 round.
Round 1: *K1, M1L, k7 (8, 9, 10), M1L, k1, pm; rep from * once more. *4 sts inc; 22 (24, 26, 28) sts.* Second marker indicates the end of the round. If your stitches are divided equally across two needle tips, the markers may be omitted since they would fall at the end of each needle.
Round 2: Knit.
Round 3: *K1, M1L, knit to 1 st before the marker, M1L, k1, slm; rep from * once more. *4 sts inc.*
Rep last 2 rounds a further 8 (9, 11, 13) times. *36 (40, 48, 56) sts inc; 58 (64, 74, 84) sts.*
Move to step 2 for charted instructions or step 3 for written instructions.

2 FOOT – CHARTED INSTRUCTIONS

Round 1: K0 (2, 4, 6), work across 28 sts from row 1 of chart, knit to end.

Last round sets chart pattern, continue to work from chart until foot measures 6 (6.5, 7.5, 8.5) cm [2½ (2¾, 3, 3½) in] less than desired foot length.

Move to step 4.

3 FOOT – WRITTEN INSTRUCTIONS

Round 1: K0 (2, 4, 6), *p2, 1/1 RPT, p2, k1 tbl, p2, 1/1 LPT, p2*, 1/1 RT, rep from * to * once more, knit to end.

Round 2: K0 (2, 4, 6), p1, 1/1 RPT, p3, k1 tbl, p3, (1/1 LPT, 1/1 RPT) twice, p3, k1 tbl, p3, 1/1 LPT, p1, knit to end.

Round 3: K0 (2, 4, 6), p1, (k1 tbl, p4) twice, 1/1 LT, p2, 1/1 LT, (p4, k1 tbl) twice, p1, knit to end.

Round 4: K0 (2, 4, 6), p1, k1 tbl, (p3, 1/1 RPT) twice, 1/1 LPT, 1/1 RPT, (1/1 LPT, p3) twice, k1 tbl, p1, knit to end.

Round 5: K0 (2, 4, 6), p1, k1 tbl, p2, 1/1 RPT, p3, 1/1 RPT, p2, 1/1 RT, p2, 1/1 LPT, p3, 1/1 LPT, p2, k1 tbl, p1, knit to end.

Round 6: K0 (2, 4, 6), p1, k1 tbl, p1, 1/1 RPT, p3, 1/1 RPT, p2, 1/1 RPT, 1/1 LPT, p2, 1/1 LPT, p3, 1/1 LPT, p1, k1 tbl, p1, knit to end.

Round 7: K0 (2, 4, 6), p1, k1 tbl, 1/1 RPT, p4, k1 tbl, p2, 1/1 RPT, p2, 1/1 LPT, p2, k1 tbl, p4, 1/1 LPT, k1 tbl, p1, knit to end.

Round 8: K0 (2, 4, 6), p1, 1/1 RT, p5, k1 tbl, p2, k1 tbl, p4, k1 tbl, p2, k1 tbl, p5, 1/1 LT, p1, knit to end.

Round 9: K0 (2, 4, 6), p1, k1 tbl, 1/1 LPT, p4, k1 tbl, p2, 1/1 LPT, p2, 1/1 RPT, p2, k1 tbl, p4, 1/1 RPT, k1 tbl, p1, knit to end.

Round 10: K0 (2, 4, 6), p1, k1 tbl, p1, 1/1 LPT, p3, 1/1 LPT, p2, 1/1 LPT, 1/1 RPT, p2, 1/1 RPT, p3, 1/1 RPT, p1, k1 tbl, p1, knit to end.

Round 11: K0 (2, 4, 6), p1, k1 tbl, p2, 1/1 LPT, p3, 1/1 LPT, p2, 1/1 RT, p2, 1/1 RPT, p3, 1/1 RPT, p2, k1 tbl, p1, knit to end.

Round 12: K0 (2, 4, 6), p1, k1 tbl, p3, 1/1 LPT, p3, (1/1 LPT, 1/1 RPT) twice, p3, 1/1 RPT, p3, k1 tbl, p1, knit to end.

Round 13: K0 (2, 4, 6), p1, (k1 tbl, p4) twice, 1/1 LT, p2, 1/1 LT, (p4, k1 tbl) twice, p1, knit to end.

Round 14: K0 (2, 4, 6), p1, 1/1 LPT, p3, k1 tbl, p3, (1/1 RPT, 1/1 LPT) twice, p3, k1 tbl, p3, 1/1 RPT, p1, knit to end.

Round 15: K0 (2, 4, 6), p2, 1/1 LPT, p2, k1 tbl, p2, 1/1 RPT, p2, 1/1 RT, p2, 1/1 LPT, p2, k1 tbl, p2, 1/1 RPT, p2, knit to end.

Round 16: K0 (2, 4, 6), p3, 1/1 LPT, p1, k1 tbl, p1, 1/1 RPT, p2, 1/1 RPT, 1/1 LPT, p2, 1/1 LPT, p1, k1 tbl, p1, 1/1 RPT, p3, knit to end.

Round 17: K0 (2, 4, 6), p4, 1/1 LPT, k1 tbl, p1, k1 tbl, p2, 1/1 RPT, p2, 1/1 LPT, p2, k1 tbl, p1, k1 tbl, 1/1 RPT, p4, knit to end.

Round 18: K0 (2, 4, 6), p5, 1/1 LT, p1, k1 tbl, (p2, k1 tbl, p2) twice, k1 tbl, p1, 1/1 RT, p5, knit to end.

Round 19: K0 (2, 4, 6), p4, 1/1 RPT, k1 tbl, p1, k1 tbl, p2, 1/1 LPT, p2, 1/1 RPT, p2, k1 tbl, p1, k1 tbl, 1/1 LPT, p4, knit to end.

Round 20: K0 (2, 4, 6), p3, 1/1 RPT, p1, k1 tbl, p1, 1/1 LPT, p2, 1/1 LPT, 1/1 RPT, p2, 1/1 RPT, p1, k1 tbl, p1, 1/1 LPT, p3, knit to end.

These 20 rounds set twisted stitch pattern. Rep these 20 rounds until foot measures 6 (6.5, 7.5, 8.5) cm [2½ (2¾, 3, 3½) in] less than desired foot length.

Move to step 4.

4 HEEL SET-UP

Next round: K0 (2, 4, 6), work twisted stitch pattern as set over 28 sts, k0 (2, 4, 6), using waste yarn k30 (32, 38, 44), slip these 30 (32, 38, 44) sts back to left needle and, using main yarn, knit to end.

You now have 30 (32, 38, 44) sts of waste yarn in your fabric. After completion of the sock, you will return to these sts, unpick the waste yarn and work an afterthought heel.

5 LEG

Next round: K0 (2, 4, 6), work twisted stitch pattern as set, knit to end.

Continue to work as set, until leg measures approx. 15cm [6in] from waste yarn sts, ending with a pattern round 8 or 18.

6 CUFF

SIZE SMALL ONLY

Round 1: *P1, k2 tbl, p2, k2 tbl, p1, k1 tbl, p2, k1 tbl, p4, k1 tbl, p2, k1 tbl, p1, k2 tbl, p2, k2 tbl, p1, k1 tbl; rep from * once more.

CHART

TWISTED STITCH PATTERN

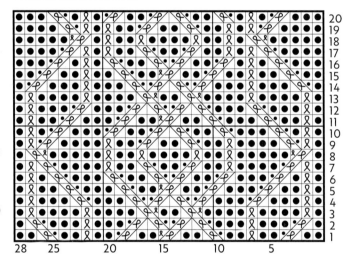

KEY

⦿ Purl

ᛉ K1 tbl

1/1 RPT slip 1 st to cable needle and hold in back, k1 tbl; p1 from cable needle

1/1 LPT slip 1 st to cable needle and hold in front, p1; k1 tbl from cable needle

1/1 RT slip 1 st to cable needle and hold in back, k1 tbl; k1 tbl from cable needle

1/1 LT slip 1 st to cable needle and hold in front, k1 tbl; k1 tbl from cable needle

December

SIZE MEDIUM ONLY
Round 1: *K2 tbl, p1, k2 tbl, p2, k2 tbl, p1, k1 tbl, p2, k1 tbl, p4, k1 tbl, p2, k1 tbl, p1, k2 tbl, p2, k2 tbl, p1, k2 tbl; rep from * once more.

SIZE LARGE ONLY
Round 1: *P2, k2 tbl, p1, k2 tbl, p2, k2 tbl, p1, k1 tbl, p2, k1 tbl, p4, k1 tbl, p2, k1 tbl, p1, k2 tbl, p2, k2 tbl, p1, k2 tbl, p2, k1 tbl; rep from * once more.

SIZE XL ONLY
Round 1: *(K2 tbl, p2, k2 tbl, p1) twice, k1 tbl, p2, k1 tbl, p4, k1 tbl, p2, k1 tbl, p1, (k2 tbl, p2, k2 tbl, p1) twice, p1; rep from * once more.

ALL SIZES
Last round sets twisted rib. Rep last round a further 14 times. Loosely cast off all sts. A sewn cast off is a good method for toe-up socks, this is worked as follows:
Break the yarn leaving a tail of approx. 1m [1yd]. Thread the tail onto a tapestry needle. *Pass the tapestry needle through the first 2 sts on the left needle tip from right to left, then back through the first st on the left needle tip from left to right and slip that st off the needle. Rep from * until all sts are cast off.

7 AFTERTHOUGHT HEEL
Pick up the right leg (or side) of the 30 (32, 38, 44) main yarn sts under the row of waste yarn sts. Turn the sock and rep the process again, picking up the 30 (32, 38, 44) sts from the other side of the main yarn. You now have 60 (64, 76, 88) sts on your needles. Carefully remove the waste yarn, ensuring all sts are safely on your needles. Begin to work in the round as follows:
Next round: K30 (32, 38, 44), pick up and knit 2 sts in the gap between sole and instep, k30 (32, 38, 44) sts, pick up and knit 2 sts in the gap between the sole and instep and pm for start of round. *64 (68, 80, 92) sts.*
Knit 6 rounds.

SIZE SMALL ONLY
Round 1 (dec): *K14, k2tog; rep from * to end. *4 sts dec; 60 sts remain.*

SIZES MEDIUM, LARGE AND XL ONLY
Round 1 (dec): *K- (32, 38, 44), k2tog; rep from * once more. *2 sts dec; - (66, 78, 90) sts remain.*

SIZE XL ONLY
Round 2: Knit.
Round 3: *K13, k2tog; rep from * to end. *6 sts dec; 84 sts remain.*
Round 4: Knit.
Round 5: *K12, k2tog; rep from * to end. *6 sts dec; 78 sts remain.*

SIZES LARGE AND XL ONLY
Round 6: Knit.
Round 7: *K11, k2tog; rep from * to end. *6 sts dec; 72 sts remain.*
Round 8: Knit.
Round 9: K10, k2tog; rep from * to end. 6 sts dec; 66 sts remain.

SIZES MEDIUM, LARGE AND XL ONLY
Round 10: Knit.
Round 11: *K9, k2tog; rep from * to end. *6 sts dec; 60 sts remain.*

ALL SIZES
Round 12: Knit.
Round 13: *K8, k2tog; rep from * to end. *6 sts dec; 54 sts remain.*
Round 14: Knit.
Round 15: *K7, k2tog; rep from * to end. *6 sts dec; 48 sts remain.*
Round 16: Knit.
Round 17: *K6, k2tog; rep from * to end. *6 sts dec; 42 sts remain.*
Round 18: Knit.
Round 19: *K5, k2tog; rep from * to end. *6 sts dec; 36 sts remain.*
Round 20: Knit.
Round 21: *K4, k2tog; rep from * to end. *6 sts dec; 30 sts remain.*
Round 22: Knit.
Round 23: *K3, k2tog; rep from * to end. *6 sts dec; 24 sts remain.*
Round 24: Knit.
Round 25: *K2, k2tog; rep from * to end. *6 sts dec; 18 sts remain.*
Round 26: *K1, k2tog; rep from * to end. *6 sts dec; 12 sts remain.*
Round 27: *K2tog; rep from * to end. *6 sts dec; 6 sts remain.*
Break yarn, leaving a 15cm [6in] tail. Thread tail through remaining sts and pull tightly to close the heel.

8 FINISHING
Weave in all ends but do not trim.
Soak your socks in lukewarm water and wool wash for 20 minutes. Squeeze out excess water (but do not wring). Press between towels to dry further. Lay your socks flat to dry, or stretch over sock blockers. When they are completely dry, trim any remaining ends.

TECHNIQUE
DOMINANCE IN FAIR ISLE KNITTING

One of the easiest ways to neaten your Fair Isle knitting is to master which way round you hold your yarns. Fair Isle involves carrying both of your yarns across the entire row (or round), in contrast to intarsia (see April's tutorial on page 16) where you work with discrete blocks of colour. The yarn not in use is carried at the rear of the work, creating floats. When you knit across a row with two colours, you have a choice as to whether your new yarn comes from above or below the previous colour. When the new yarn comes from above, the stitch you create will be slightly shorter than if you bring the new yarn from below the previous colour. The difference is very small, but over a large piece of knitted fabric, the effect can be very noticeable.

In the swatch pictures to the right, you can see the effect of holding the yellow below the grey (1), holding the grey below the yellow (2) and being inconsistent in which way round the yarns are held (3). Swatch 1 shows how the slightly longer yellow stitches make the patterning really stand out. In swatch 2 the patterning is neat but less dominant, and in swatch 3, the yarns have been held in a mixture of ways, and you can see that the effect is untidy. The difference is most obvious when you compare the single stitch motifs in the zigzags at top and bottom, but across the project as a whole, you would definitely notice if one mitten was knitted like swatch 1, with the second one knitted with the yarns held the other way round.

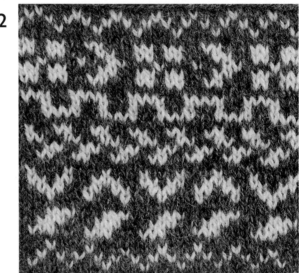

IDENTIFYING FOREGROUND AND BACKGROUND COLOURS
Before starting work on a section of Fair Isle patterning, decide which colour(s) will be your foreground and which will be background. In many patterns, this will be obvious – in Ella's Shaila mittens, the yellow is the foreground and the dark grey is the background colour – but in others you may need to make a judgement call. Try to avoid changing a colour from foreground to background within a motif. Throughout this tutorial I have assumed that you will want your foreground colour to be strongest (and have the slightly larger stitches), but it is of course entirely possible that you want your patterning to be less punchy, in which case you just need to hold your yarns the opposite way round.

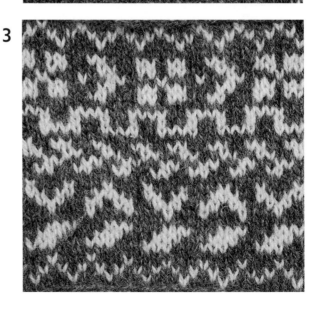

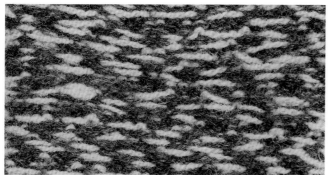

ABOVE: *Inconsistent stranding*

HOW DO YOU HOLD YOUR YARNS?

For single colour projects do you hold your yarn in your left or right hand? Are you dominantly left- or right-handed? Are you already familiar with an alternative knitting style? These are all questions to consider when you decide how to hold your yarns for Fair Isle work. In the tutorial below I explain how to work with two colours in three different ways. There are many other alternatives, including methods where you let go of the yarn not in use,

and they are all perfectly acceptable (we are not the knitting police!). The key is to ensure that you are consistent in how the foreground and background colours are picked up. If you are new to Fair Isle knitting, I would recommend practising one of the methods outlined below for the simple reason that if you are holding both yarns all the time, you can only be consistent. It isn't possible to mistakenly take the background colour from below if it's always being held in the "above" position.

GENERAL PRINCIPLES

The foreground colour is always held to the left and behind the background colour. This ensures that the background always passes over the foreground, thus keeping the foreground stitches slightly longer. When you work consistently like this, the two balls of yarn should never tangle. If you find that your yarns are getting twisted together, then stop and look back at the floats of yarn on the wrong side of the fabric. You should be able to see if there are points where you are picking up the yarns the wrong way round. On the wrong side of my mitten (4, below), you can see that on each row the yellow floats sit below the grey floats. On the wrong side of a swatch where I mixed how my yarns were held, the floats are angled and you can see that it isn't consistent (above, left).

HOLDING BOTH YARNS IN YOUR RIGHT HAND

This is my preferred method. I'm strongly right-handed, and although I can knit with the yarn in my left hand, I am faster and more comfortable with both yarns in my right hand.

i Hold your background yarn over your index finger and your foreground yarn over your middle finger.

ii Use your middle finger to knit the stitches in the foreground colour. Notice how this brings the yarn below the background yarn.

TIP

There are many, many tips and tricks for working Fair Isle knitting, but keeping your background and foreground colours held consistently is one of the easiest to master, and makes a huge impact on the neatness and overall look of your finished project.

iii Work in pattern as directed and when you next need to work a stitch in the background colour, use your index finger to work that stitch. Notice how the yarn comes above the foreground.

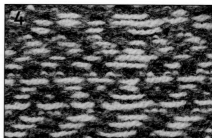

While you continue to work with the yarns on your index and middle fingers in this way, you will always be bringing the new yarn correctly under or over the old one. If you turn your work inside out, you can see that the foreground floats (yellow) are always below the background floats (grey).

HOLDING ONE YARN IN EACH HAND

This is a very popular way to hold two yarns for Fair Isle knitting – you hold the background colour in your right hand, with the foreground yarn in your left hand. As required by your pattern, you alternate between using your index fingers on each hand.

i To work a stitch in the foreground colour, dip the right needle tip behind the yarn on your left index finger and scoop it through the stitch (this method is sometimes called picking because you use the needle to pick up the yarn). Notice how the foreground yarn passes underneath the background yarn.

ii To work a stitch in the background colour, use your right index finger to wrap the yarn around the right needle tip (this method is sometimes called throwing because you use your index finger to throw the yarn around the needle). Notice how the yarn comes above the foreground.

HOLDING BOTH YARNS IN YOUR LEFT HAND

If you already knit with your yarn held in your left hand, or you are more dominantly left-handed, you may find this the easiest method to learn.
Hold both yarns over your left index finger, with the foreground colour to the left, and the background colour to the right.

i To knit a stitch in the background colour, scoop the needle around the background yarn and pull it through the stitch. The background colour comes from above the foreground colour.

ii To knit a stitch in the foreground colour, pass the needle tip between the yarns and pick up the foreground colour, pulling it through your stitch. The foreground colour comes from below the background colour.

> **TERMINOLOGY: FAIR ISLE vs STRANDED COLOURWORK**
> The term Fair Isle should only be applied to stranded colourwork motifs originating from the island of Fair Isle, although the term is often used generically for all stranded colourwork. This month's mitten pattern by Ella Gordon features peerie motifs found in Fair Isle knitting, so I have referred to it as Fair Isle throughout this chapter, but all of the techniques can equally be applied to any stranded colourwork project. As a rule of thumb, all Fair Isle is stranded, but not all stranded colourwork should be called Fair Isle.

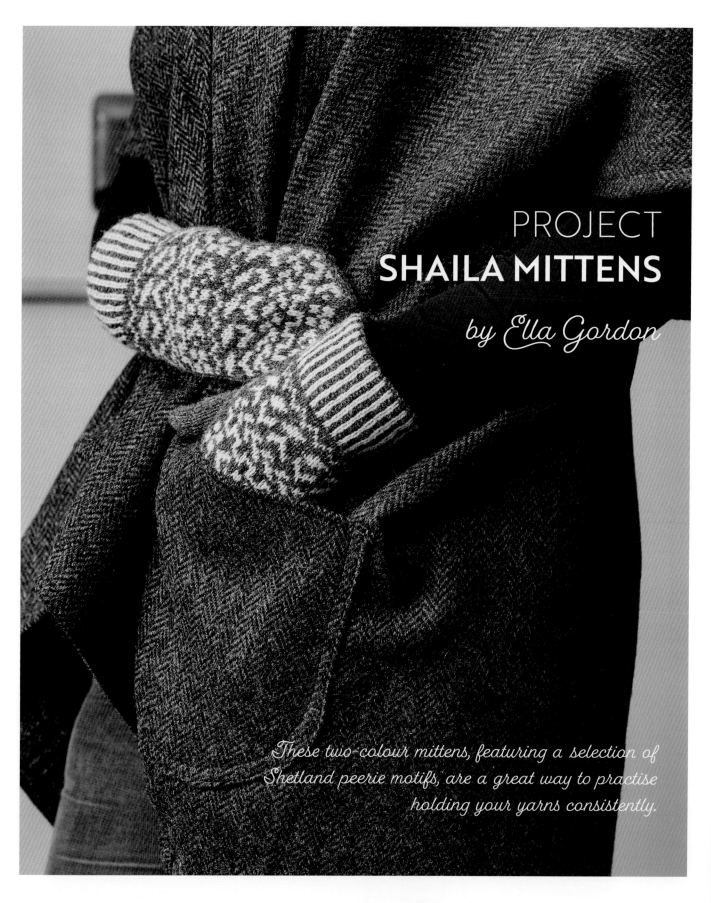

PROJECT
SHAILA MITTENS

by Ella Gordon

These two-colour mittens, featuring a selection of Shetland peerie motifs, are a great way to practise holding your yarns consistently.

SIZES

Small (Large)
Finished circumference above thumb: 18 (21) cm [7¼ (8¼) in]
Mitten length from cuff to top: 22 (25) cm [8¾ (9¾) in]

YARN

Jamieson & Smith 2ply Jumper Weight (4ply weight / fingering; 100% Shetland wool; 115m per 25g ball)
Yarn A: Shade 23; 2 x 25g balls both sizes
Yarn B: Shade 54; 2 x 25g balls both sizes

NEEDLES AND NOTIONS

1 set 2.5mm [US 1.5] double-pointed needles or needles suitable for your preferred method of small circumference knitting, or one size smaller than those needed to match tension
1 set 3mm [US 2.5] double-pointed needles or needles suitable for your preferred method of small circumference knitting, or size needed to match tension
2 stitch markers
2 lengths smooth waste yarn for afterthought thumb placement
Latch hook tool or crochet hook (optional)

TENSION

34 sts and 37 rounds to 10cm [4in] over chart patterns using 3mm needles, after washing and blocking

TECHNIQUES

These mittens use the afterthought thumb method as described in December's tutorial (page 92).

ABBREVIATIONS

A full list of abbreviations appears on the inside back cover.

PATTERN NOTES

These mittens feature an extra-warm folded cuff with a plain inside and corrugated rib on the outside. The hands showcase a selection of peerie (small) colourwork motifs allowing you to practise holding your yarns consistently. To help you keep your floats even, it is recommended that you turn your knitting inside out for the colourwork sections. This forces the floats around the outside of the work and keeps them from puckering the fabric. It is only necessary to weave in the floats if they are carried over more than 5 stitches. The mittens are knitted in the round with an afterthought thumb.

CHART NOTES

Read all chart rows from right to left.

January

MITTENS

1 CUFF

With yarn A, smaller needles and the long-tail method, loosely cast on 58 (70) sts. Join to work in the round, taking care not to twist sts, and pm for start of round.
Knit 20 (26) rounds.
Join in yarn B, but do not break yarn A.
Next round: With yarn B, knit.
Next round: With yarn B, purl.
Round 1: *K1A, p1B; rep from * to end.
Rep last round a further 19 (25) times.
Change to larger needles.
Next round (inc): With yarn B, *k1, M1L, k28 (34), M1L; rep from * once more. *4 sts inc, 62 (74) sts.*

2 LEFT HAND

You may find it helpful to place an additional marker after st 31 (37) to mark the halfway point.
Round 1: Work across 31 (37) sts of chart A (B) twice.
Last round sets chart A (B) pattern. Continue to work from chart as set until chart row 16 (14) is complete. Do not break yarn A on the plain rows between motifs.

3 SET-UP LEFT THUMB AND COMPLETE HAND

Next round: Work as set to last 12 (14) sts, using waste yarn k8 (10), slip 8 (10) sts just worked back to left needle, then work as set to end of round.
You now have 8 (10) sts of waste yarn in your fabric. After completion of the mitten, you will return to these sts, unpick the waste yarn and work an afterthought thumb.

Continue to work from chart A (B) as set until chart row 60 (66) is complete, decreasing as indicated. *42 (50) sts dec, 20 (24) sts remain.*
Slip the first 10 (12) sts to another needle. Break yarn B, leaving a 30cm [12in] tail and graft the two sets of sts together using Kitchener stitch.

4 AFTERTHOUGHT THUMB

Using larger needles, pick up the right leg (or side) of the 8 (10) main yarn sts under the row of waste yarn sts. Turn the mitten and pick up 8 (10) main yarn sts above the waste yarn in the same way. You now have 16 (20) sts on your needles. Carefully remove the waste yarn, ensuring all sts are safely on your needles. *16 (20) sts.*
With yarn B, knit until thumb measures 5 (6) cm [2 (2¼) in].
Next round: [K2tog] 8 (10) times. *8 (10) sts dec; 8 (10) sts remain.*
Next round: Knit.
Next round: [K2tog] 4 (5) times. *4 (5) sts dec; 4 (5) sts remain.*
Break yarn and fasten off through remaining sts, pull through to inside of thumb and pull tight again to ensure the tip isn't too pointed.

5 RIGHT MITTEN

Work steps 1 and 2 as for left mitten, following chart C (D), rather than A (B).
Next round: Work across 4 sts from row 17 (15) of chart, using waste yarn k8 (10), slip 8 (10) sts just worked back to left needle, then work as set to end of round.
You now have 8 (10) sts of waste yarn in your fabric. After completion of the mitten, you will return to these sts, unpick the waste yarn and work an afterthought thumb.
Continue to work from chart C (D) as set until chart row 60 (66) is complete, decreasing as indicated. *42 (50) sts dec, 20 (24) sts remain.*
Break yarn B and, using a tapestry needle, graft the two sides together using Kitchener stitch.
Work step 4 as for left mitten.

6 FINISHING

Turn mittens inside out and weave in ends. Fold over the double cuff and, using yarn A, sew the cast-on edge to the inside matching each cast-on st to the floats of the last row of corrugated rib.
If desired, you can avoid your fingertips getting caught in the floats at the tips of the mittens by latching the floats of yarn A as follows:
Take a latch hook tool or crochet hook and insert your chosen tool into the top float and pull through each float below it as far as required. On the last stitch hook through a length of yarn and tie in a knot before weaving in the ends.
Soak your mittens in lukewarm water and wool wash for 20 minutes. Carefully remove excess water by squeezing (not wringing) and press between towels. Lay your mittens flat or place on mitten blockers. Leave to dry. Trim any remaining ends.

KEY

☐ Using yarn A (23); knit

■ Using yarn B (54); knit

◹ Using shade indicated; ssk

◺ Using shade indicated; k2tog

15/17 Refer to instructions for this round

▬ Thumb placement

CHART B
LARGE, LEFT MITTEN

CHART A
SMALL, LEFT MITTEN

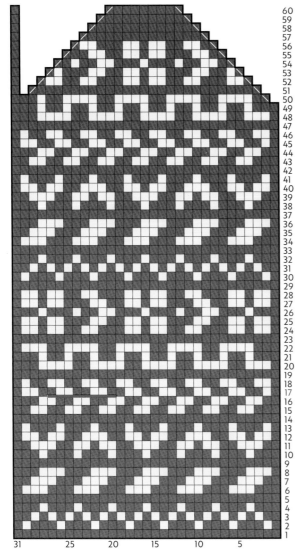

January

KEY

☐ Using yarn A (23); knit

■ Using yarn B (54); knit

◩ Using shade indicated; ssk

◪ Using shade indicated; k2tog

15/17 Refer to instructions for this round

▬ Thumb placement

CHART D
LARGE, RIGHT MITTEN

CHART C
SMALL, RIGHT MITTEN

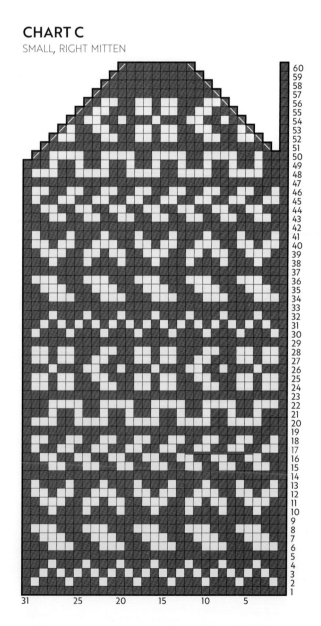

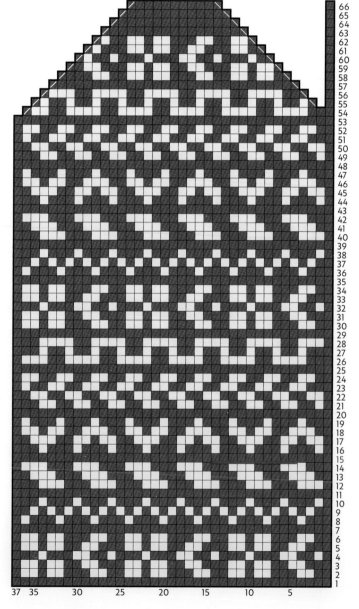

TECHNIQUE
STEEKS

Few techniques seem to fill knitters with more fear than steeks. The idea of taking your scissors to your knitting just sounds like a terrible idea. That is, until you actually do it.

WHAT IS A STEEK?

Steeks are most commonly found in stranded colourwork (or Fair Isle) projects. A steek is a small bridge of stitches, rather like the seam allowance in a sewing pattern, that allows you to knit a project in the round, and then cut it open at a later date to create flat pieces. This has benefits over working back and forth, since you are always working from the right side of the knitting. This makes it easier to spot errors, and avoids having to purl the colourwork pattern. It also means that you don't need to sew in your ends. You can simply change colour in the centre of the steek, and then once you've cut open your steek, you can just trim away the knots and any stray ends.

THE IMPORTANCE OF YARN CHOICE

The key to successful steeking is choice of yarn. If you use a sticky, woollen yarn, like a woollen-spun Shetland yarn (such as the Jamieson & Smith 2ply Jumper Weight that's used in this month's pattern), all you need to do is cut open the steek. No reinforcement is required since the yarn sticks to itself and won't unravel. Whereas using a worsted-spun superwash merino wool, or worse, a slippery fibre such as silk or cotton, will make the chances of success far lower (in the case of 100% cotton or silk, just don't do it!). The stickier (or more felt-able) the yarn, the more stable the steek will be.

REINFORCING YOUR STEEK

Whilst it's entirely possible to just cut open your steek, pick up and knit on your edgings, and leave the cut edges to gently felt together over time, most knitters err on the side of caution. And who wouldn't, given the amount of time that is invested in knitting even a small steeked project? If you've knitted an entire garment, then it's only natural to want to be completely sure that your steek will behave itself. The best way to be certain is to knit a steeked swatch and try out your method before you commit to the finished garment. There are a number of different methods available for reinforcing a steek: Working rows of crochet each side of the centre stitch(es) prior to cutting; machine sewing along each side of the cut line; hand sewing along each side of the cut line; and, finally, cutting with no reinforcement, but then sewing down the resulting edges (which is not the strongest method, but more than sufficient for a sticky yarn).

The crochet method is good for reasonably sticky yarns, whereas if you are using a soft, superwash yarn, or something with more slippery fibres, then a machine or hand sewn reinforcement will be necessary. Below you will find stepwise instructions for cutting a steek without reinforcement, and crochet reinforcement of a steek. In the Extra Resources section on page 115 you will also find links to online instructions on sewing steek reinforcements.

The steeks in Mary Jane Mucklestone's sweet Oorik tank top are 8 stitches wide. She uses stripes of colours that create a centre line of two pattern colour stitches. The steek will be cut open between these 2 stitches.

STEPWISE INSTRUCTIONS FOR CROCHET REINFORCEMENT OF A STEEK

Use a yarn of similar thickness to your main yarn (unless your main yarn is really bulky, in which case use a finer yarn). I am using Jamieson & Smith 2ply Jumper Weight in a contrasting colour.

i Carefully identify the centre stitch(es) of your steek. In this month's pattern there are 2 central stitches in the steek.

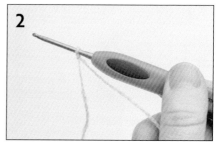

ii Make a slip knot on your crochet hook.

iii Starting at the bottom of your steek, pass your crochet hook under one leg of the left-hand centre stitch, and one leg of the adjacent stitch.

iv Wrap your yarn around the hook.

v Pull the yarn through the stitches. You now have 2 loops on your hook.

vi Pull the yarn through the slip knot. You now only have 1 loop on your hook.

vii Move 1 stitch up the steek and repeat steps iii-vi.

viii Continue to work up the steek in the same way, until you reach the cast-off edge.

ix Cut yarn leaving a short tail, and pull through the final stitch.

x Turn your knitting through 180°, ready to work back down the opposite side of the steek. Follow steps ii-vii as for the first side of the steek.

xi Fasten off the final stitch, leaving 2 rows of crochet each side of the centre stitches.

xii Carefully cut between the centre stitches of the steek. This step isn't nearly as scary as it sounds.

xiii The crochet reinforcement keeps the edge neat.

TIP
If the stitches at the base of your steek are all in one colour it can be hard to see which legs you should be crocheting together. It helps to look further up the steek, where the stitches are in two colours. Work out which legs you should be passing the hook under, then follow the columns down to the base of the steek.

STEPWISE INSTRUCTIONS FOR CUTTING AN UNREINFORCED STEEK

i With a sticky Shetland yarn, there is no need to reinforce your steek; you can simply cut it open.

ii The cut edge is remarkably stable – knitting doesn't unravel sideways nearly as easily as you would imagine .

STEPWISE INSTRUCTIONS FOR FINISHING YOUR STEEKED EDGE

i Pick up and knit stitches between the last steek stitch and the first pattern stitch, as directed in your pattern (1 and 2).

ii Work your edging as indicated in the pattern (often a rib is added at the neck or armholes where a steek is cut).

iii Once the edging is in progress, the cut steek edge lies naturally to the back of the work.

iv You can trim the steek edge back to neaten it, if desired.

v The steek edge can be sewn down with a whipstitch to secure it, if desired.

PROJECT
OORIK TANK TOP

by Mary-Jane Mucklestone

*Worked entirely in the round, this sweet
little tank top uses steek bridges to create the
arm and neck openings.*

SIZES

Approximate age: 6 (12, 24) months
To fit chest: 43 (48, 53) cm [17 (19, 20¾) in]
Finished chest size: 48 (53, 57.5) cm [19 (20¾, 22¾) in]
Total length: 29 (31.5, 34) cm [11¼ (12½, 13¼) in]
Length to armhole: 19 (21, 21) cm [7½ (8¼, 8¼) in]
Armhole depth: 10 (10.5, 13) cm [4 (4¼, 5) in]
Back neck width: 8.5 (9, 9) cm [3¼ (3½, 3½) in]
Shown in largest size.

YARN

Jamieson & Smith Shetland Supreme Jumper Weight (4ply /
fingering weight; 100% Shetland wool; 172m per 50g ball)
Yarn A: Gaulmogot (2006); 1 x 50g ball all sizes
Jamieson & Smith 2ply Jumper Weight (4ply / fingering
weight; 100% Shetland wool; 115m per 25g ball)
Yarn B: Shade FC15; 1 (1, 2) x 25g balls
Yarn C: Shade 9144; 1 x 25g ball all sizes
Yarn D: Shade 66; 1 x 25g ball all sizes

NEEDLES AND NOTIONS

1 set 2.5mm [US 1.5] circular needles, 40cm [16in] long, or your
preferred needles for knitting in the round
1 set 3.25mm [US 3] circular needles, 40cm [16in] long, or your
preferred needles for knitting in the round
Stitch markers of different colours
Stitch holders or waste yarn
Tapestry needle
T-pins for blocking
Sharp scissors
Crochet hook of a similar size to the main knitting needles
for crocheted steeks (optional)

TENSION

25 sts and 30 rounds to 10cm [4in] over Fair Isle stocking
stitch, using 3.25mm needles, after washing and blocking

ABBREVIATIONS

A full list of abbreviations appears on the inside back cover.

SWATCHING

Knitting a swatch allows you to practise cutting the steek
before embarking on the whole project, as well as letting you
check you are achieving the correct tension.
Using yarn A and larger needles, cast on 57 sts. Join to work in
the round, taking care not to twist. Pm for start of round.
Round 1: Work across row 1 of chart A.
Last round sets chart pattern. Continue to work from chart A
until chart row 15 is complete.
Cast off all sts.
Following the instructions in the photo tutorial, reinforce
your steek using crochet (optional), or simply cut the steek
between the centre sts (at the start of the round).

TECHNIQUES

Please refer back to January's tutorial (page 99) on managing
dominance in Fair Isle knitting.

BACKWARDS LOOP CAST ON

*Wrap yarn around left thumb from front to back and secure
in palm with other fingers. Insert needle upwards through
strand on thumb. Slip loop from thumb onto right needle,
pulling yarn to tighten. Rep from * for desired number of sts.

STRIPE PATTERN FOR STEEKS

Work steek sts in vertical stripes every round as [k1
background colour, k1 foreground colour] twice, [k1
foreground colour, k1 background colour] twice. This
provides a clear 2 st centre line in foreground colour for
cutting the steeks open, and also a clear, unobtrusive edge
in background colour for picking up neckband and sleeve
edging.

PATTERN NOTES

The body is worked entirely in the round to the shoulders,
using steeks for the armholes and front and back necks. The
edging and neckband are worked in the round by picking up
stitches and working 1x1 rib. You can customise the length
of your vest by adding pattern rounds before casting on for
steeks.

CHART NOTES

Read all chart rows from right to left.

KEY

☐ Using yarn A
(Gaulmogot); knit

▨ Using yarn B
(FC15); knit

▩ Using yarn C
(9144); knit

CHART A SWATCH

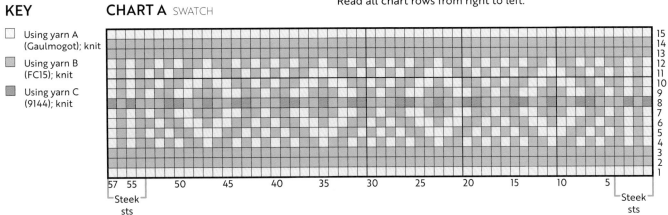

February

TANK TOP

BODY
1 CAST ON AND WORK RIBBING
With smaller needles and yarn A, cast on 120 (132, 144) sts. Join for working in the round, being careful not to twist. Pm for start of round.
Round 1: *K1, p1; rep from * to end of round.
Last round sets 1x1 rib pattern. Continue to work in 1x1 rib pattern for 3.5cm [1½in].

2 FAIR ISLE CHART
Change to larger needles and work chart B (C, D) as follows, changing yarns as indicated:
Round 1: [Work across 12 sts from row 1 of chart B (C, D)] 10 (11, 12) times.
Last round sets chart B (C, D) pattern. Continue to work from chart B (C, D) as set until you have completed chart row 46 (6, 6) for the first (second, second) time (46 (52, 52) rounds in chart pattern).
Break yarns.

3 SET UP STEEKS AND SHAPE ARMHOLES AND NECKLINE
Throughout the next section, keep the chart B (C, D) pattern correct as set (ensuring that the motifs continue to line up correctly as you work the shaping). Cast on all steek sts using the backwards loop method, then work steek sts in the following pattern throughout: [K1 background colour, k1 foreground colour] twice, [k1 foreground colour, k1 background colour] twice. Where only one colour is used in a round, simply k8 steek sts.

SIZE SMALL ONLY
Next round: Remove start of round marker, slip next 3 sts to a st holder, using yarn A, cast on 4 steek sts, pm, pattern 26 sts, place next st on a locking st marker or st holder (centre front st), pm, cast on 8 steek sts, pm, pattern 26 sts, pm, slip next 7 sts to a stitch holder for underarm, cast on 8 steek sts, pm, pattern 53 sts, then slip final 4 sts to the same st holder as the 3 sts from the start of round, pm, cast on 4 steek sts, pm for start of round. *105 body sts and 2 sets of 7 underarm sts on holders; body sts comprise 26 sts for each front and 53 back sts; plus 3 steeks of 8 sts each.*

MEDIUM AND LARGE SIZES ONLY
Next round: Remove start of round marker, slip next – (3, 4) sts to a st holder, join in yarn C with a slip knot and cast on a further 3 steek sts alternating yarns B and C, pm, pattern – (29, 31) sts, place next st on a locking st marker or st holder (centre front st), pm, cast on 8 steek sts, pm, pattern – (29, 31) sts, pm, slip next – (7, 9) sts to a stitch holder for underarm, cast on 8 steek sts, pm, pattern – (59, 63) sts, then slip final – (4, 5) sts to the same st holder as the – (3, 4) sts from the start of round, pm, cast on 4 steek sts, pm for start of round. *– (117, 125) body sts and 2 sets of – (7, 9) underarm sts on holders; body sts comprise – (29, 31) sts for each front and – (59, 63) back sts; plus 3 steeks of 8 sts each.*

SCHEMATIC

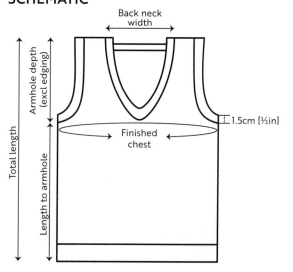

Back neck width

Armhole depth (excl edging)

Total length

Length to armhole

Finished chest

1.5cm [½in]

ALL SIZES

Read through the following steps but do **NOT** work them. Then follow the instructions for your size, telling you which combination of steps A-D you need to work.

Step A (dec armholes and front neck): *K4 steek sts, slm, k2tog, pattern to 2 sts before marker, ssk, slm, k4 steek sts; rep from * twice more. *6 sts dec.*

Step B: K4 steek sts, [slm, pattern to marker, slm, k8 steek sts] twice, slm, pattern to marker, slm, k4 steek sts.

Step C (dec at front neck): K4 steek sts, slm, pattern to 2 sts before marker, ssk, slm, k8 steek sts, slm, k2tog, pattern to marker, slm, k8 steek sts, slm, pattern to marker, slm, k4 steek sts. *2 sts dec.*

Step D (dec at armholes): K4 steek sts, slm, k2tog, pattern to marker, slm, k8 steek sts, slm, pattern to 2 sts before marker, ssk, slm, k8 steek sts, slm, k2tog, pattern to 2 sts before marker, ssk, slm, k4 steek sts. *4 sts dec.*

Size Small only: Work step A 3 times. [Work step B then step A] twice. Work step B then step C. Work step B then step A. [Work step B twice, then step C] twice. Work step B 3 times, then work step C. *44 sts dec; 61 body sts remain; body sts comprise 10 sts for each front and 41 back sts; plus 3 steeks of 8 sts each.*

Size Medium only: Work step A 3 times. [Work step B then step A] twice. Work step B then step C. Work step B then step A. [Work step B twice, then step C] twice. [Work step B 3 times, then work step C] twice. *46 sts dec; 71 body sts remain; body sts comprise 12 sts for each front and 47 back sts; plus 3 steeks of 8 sts each.*

Size Large only: Work step A 3 times. [Work step B then step A] twice. Work step B then step C. Work step B then step A. Work step B twice, then step C, then step D. Work step B then step C. [Work step B 3 times, then work step C] twice. *50 sts dec; 75 body sts remain; body sts comprise 13 sts for each front and 49 back sts; plus 3 steeks of 8 sts each.*

ALL SIZES

Work step B a further 3 (1, 6) times. You should now have completed chart B (C, D) row 25 (33, 38) for the second time.

4 SHAPE BACK NECK

Next round: K4 steek sts, [slm, pattern to marker, slm, k8 steek sts] twice, slm, pattern 10 (12, 13) sts, cast off next 21 (23, 23) sts for back neck, pattern to marker, slm, k4 steek sts. *40 (48, 52) body sts remain; 4 sets of 10 (12, 13) shoulder sts; plus 3 steeks of 8 sts each.*

Next round: K4 steek sts, [slm, pattern to marker, slm, k8 steek sts] twice, slm, pattern to cast-off sts, pm, cast on 8 steek sts, pm, pattern to marker, slm, k4 steek sts. *40 (48, 52) body sts; 4 sets of 10 (12, 13) shoulder sts; plus 4 steeks of 8 sts each.*

Next round: *K4 steek sts, slm, pattern to marker, slm, k4 steek sts; rep from * a further 3 times.

Rep last round a further 1 (1, 3) times.

Next round: K4 steek sts, [remove marker, pattern to marker, remove marker, cast off 8 steek sts] 4 times (final steek cast off will pass end of round marker, which can be removed). *4 sets of 10 (12, 13) shoulder sts remain.*

5 REINFORCE AND CUT STEEKS

Turn garment inside out and join shoulders by working a 3-needle cast off as follows:

Slip front shoulder sts to one needle tip and back shoulder sts to a second needle tip. Using a 3rd needle, knit together the first stitch from front and rear needles. *Knit together the next stitch from each needle (2 sts on your right needle), cast off 1 stitch; rep from * across shoulder. Break yarn and fasten off.

Rep for second shoulder.

Refer to photo tutorial for more detail on finishing your steeks. If desired, reinforce steeks by crochet. Cut steeks carefully between the two centre stitches.

6 NECKBAND

With RS facing and using smaller circular needle and yarn A, beginning at left shoulder seam, pick up and knit 30 (32, 38) sts evenly spaced along left side of front neck between body and steek sts, knit the held st at centre front, mark this stitch with a locking st marker or safety pin, pick up and knit 30 (32, 38) sts evenly spaced along right side of front neck to shoulder seam, pick up and knit 3 (3, 5) sts down to back neck cast-off sts, pick up and knit 21 (23, 23) sts across back neck cast-off edge, pick up and knit 3 (3, 5) sts to shoulder seam. Pm and join for working in the round. *88 (94, 110) sts.*

Next round: [K1, p1] 14 (15, 18) times, k1, cdd (removing locking st marker and replacing it on this centre st), *k1, p1; rep from * to end. *2 sts dec; 86 (92, 108) sts remain.*

Next round: Work in rib to 1 st before marked centre st, cdd (removing locking st marker and replacing it on this centre st), rib to end as set. *2 sts dec.*

Rep last round a further 4 times. *10 sts dec; 76 (82, 98) sts.*

Cast off in rib patt.

7 ARMHOLE EDGINGS (WORK BOTH ALIKE)

With RS facing and using smaller circular needle and yarn A, beginning at the end of the underarm sts, pick up and knit 28 (31, 36) sts evenly to shoulder seam, pick up and knit 1 st in shoulder seam, pick up and knit 28 (31, 36) sts evenly to underarm, knit across 7 (7, 9) sts from underarm st holder. Pm and join for working in the round. *64 (70, 82) sts.*

Work 1x1 rib as set in step 1 for a total of 5 rounds. Cast off all sts in rib patt.

8 FINISHING

Weave in all ends. Trim waste steek sts neatly and fold to WS. Tack down steek edges with whipstitch if desired. Soak your tank top in lukewarm water and wool wash for 20 minutes. Carefully remove excess water by squeezing (not wringing) and press between towels. Lay your tank top flat and leave to dry. Trim any remaining ends.

Charts appear overleaf.

February

KEY

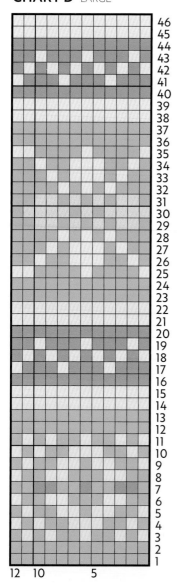

Using yarn A
(Gaulmogot); knit

Using yarn B
(FC15); knit

Using yarn C
(9144); knit

Using yarn D
(66); knit

CHART D LARGE

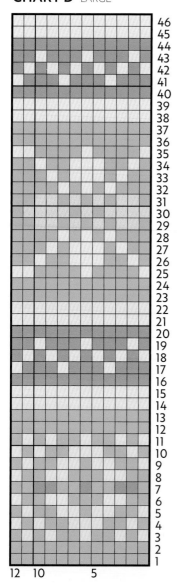

CHART C MEDIUM

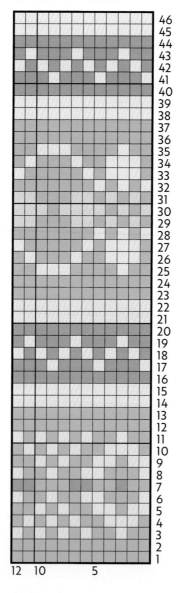

CHART B SMALL

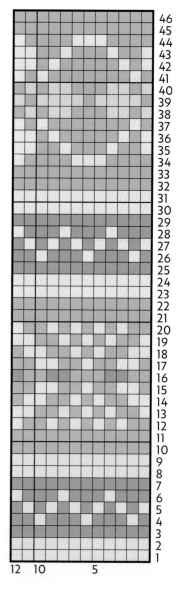

INFORMATION

EXTRA RESOURCES

A general book on knitting techniques will answer many of your basic questions. I would recommend having at least one or two of the following on your shelves:

The Principles of Knitting by June Hemmons Hiatt
Touchstone, 2012
The Knowledgeable Knitter by Margaret Radcliffe
Storey Publishing, 2014
The Handknitter's Handbook by Montse Stanley
David & Charles, 1986
Knitting Without Tears by Elizabeth Zimmermann
Simon & Schuster, 1971

TENSION

Tension (US gauge) information is given for all projects. If you don't match tension with the recommended needle size, try again with smaller or larger needles as required. Yarn quantity used and finished size are determined by matching tension correctly.

TECHNIQUES

The following techniques are used in this book, and you may find these online tutorials helpful:

STOCKING STITCH GRAFTING (KITCHENER STITCH)
www.woollywormhead.com/grafting/

I-CORD
www.purlsoho.com/create/i-cord/

CABLING WITHOUT A CABLE NEEDLE
blog.ysolda.com/ysolda-blog/2014/5/8/technique-thursday-cabling-without-a-cable-needle

SEWING STEEK REINFORCEMENTS
twostrands.com/2015/12/21/top-10-tips-for-machine-sewn-steeks/

STYLING

The majority of the clothes used for styling are from Boden.
www.boden.co.uk

YARNS

Many thanks to the following companies for providing yarn support:

Fyberspates and Coop Knits   *www.fyberspates.co.uk*

Schoppel Wolle   *www.schoppel-wolle.de/en*

Jamieson & Smith   *www.shetlandwoolbrokers.co.uk*

We stock the full range of yarns used in *A Year of Techniques* in our online shop: **www.acknitwear.co.uk**

WHERE TO FIND US?

You can follow Jen and Jim on...

RAVELRY   **JenACKnitwear / VeufTricot**
FACEBOOK   **Arnall-Culliford Knitwear**
INSTAGRAM   **@jenacknitwear / @veuftricot**
TWITTER   **@jenacknitwear / @veuftricot**
YOUTUBE   **JenACKnitwear**
OUR BLOG   **www.acknitwear.co.uk/blog**

SUPPORT

If you require help with any of the techniques, or patterns, do join us in the knitalong threads on Ravelry at Arnall-Culliford Knitwear (**www.ravelry.com/groups/arnall-culliford-knitwear**) or in The Lounge (**forums.masondixonknitting.com**). You may find your question has already been asked, and if not, there are lots of helpful and friendly knitters around to assist you. Your question may also help others, so please don't hesitate to post to the groups.

VIDEO TUTORIALS

All of the video tutorials for *A Year of Techniques* can be found at **www.acknitwear.co.uk/a-year-of-techniques-tutorials**.

HELP WITH YOUR DOWNLOADS

For technical assistance with your purchase of *A Year of Techniques*, please email jim@acknitwear.co.uk.

THE TEAM

JEN ARNALL-CULLIFORD

In demand as a meticulous editor of knitting patterns for others, Jen is sometimes tempted into creating her own designs. She has an encyclopaedic knowledge of knitting techniques, and has written all of the tutorials in this volume.

JIM ARNALL-CULLIFORD

Jim is somewhat bemused by the turn life has taken of late – editing and designing knitwear wasn't where he thought his chemistry degree would lead him! Jim is the brains behind this book's concept.

NIC BLACKMORE **Art and Production Editor**

Nic has guided the look and feel of *A Year of Techniques*, providing advice on all aspects of its design. She is also the best virtual office mate in the world.

JESSE WILD **Photographer**

When he isn't photographing cycling and rock legends, Jesse can be found ensuring every stitch of the knitwear is in focus, and filming our video tutorials. His creative eye for the best spot for a photo has been invaluable. *www.jessewild.co.uk*

SALLY SOMERS **Chief Knit-picker**

Between teaching kids how to checkmate with a lawnmower and bringing consistency and clarity to the nation's cookbooks, Sally has found time to turn her hand to knitting, and combed the text of this book for anomalies.

BRISTOL IVY challenges the way in which techniques are used, and pushes our understanding of how to manipulate knitted fabric, without ever losing sight of a stunning finished project, or joy in its creation. *www.bristolivy.com*

ELLA AUSTIN has an incredible talent for colourwork, which she often uses in her irresistible knitted toy designs. *www.ravelry.com/designers/ella-austin*

ELLA GORDON Shetland Wool Week Patron in 2016, is known both for her wonderful colourwork designs, and for her extensive collection of vintage knitwear. *ellagordon.wordpress.com*

MARTINA BEHM's patterns are the magic combination of moreishly easy to knit and interesting in construction. *strickmich.frischetexte.de/en/*

MARY JANE MUCKLESTONE has a deserved reputation as an inventive stranded colourwork specialist, and her Stopover yoked sweater was a runaway hit in February 2016. *maryjanemucklestone.com*

Entertaining to knit and amusing to wear, **RACHEL COOPEY**'s sock and accessory patterns exude joy. *www.coopknits.co.uk*

ROSEMARY (ROMI) HILL regularly stuns the knitting community with the beauty of her lace designs; her gorgeous aesthetic is instantly recognisable. *www.designsbyromi.com*

SARAH HATTON has created designs for many of the UK's leading yarn companies, and created a number of iconic garments; her fabulous patterns often feature beautiful cables and texture. *www.sarahhatton.com*

TIN CAN KNITS are famous for their baby to big sizing, extensive tutorials and colourful designs. Tin Can Knits is the creative collaboration of Emily Wessel and Alexa Ludeman. *www.tincanknits.com*

Hat architect extraordinaire, **WOOLLY WORMHEAD**'s never-ending creativity and clever constructions make her patterns hard to put down. *www.woollywormhead.com*

KAY GARDINER and **ANN SHAYNE** are the brains behind Mason-Dixon Knitting, and have championed *A Year of Techniques* since we first emailed to ask if they would consider writing the Foreword. Their willingness to jump into the unknown with us has given us courage, and their humour and generous advice has been invaluable. *www.masondixonknitting.com*

ACKNOWLEDGEMENTS

Many people contribute to the success of a book, and we are insanely grateful to everyone who has helped along the way.

Particular thanks are due to our family who have not only put up with us while we hid in the office and wrote, but also entertained our children and stepped in at the last minute to keep us from drowning in yarn.

My local knitting group are a source of constant support, cake and encouragement. Thank you not only for always listening, but also for allowing us to photograph you knitting.

Many thanks to Tabitha Clayson and Simon Morrissey, and Ed Arnall-Culliford for lending us their beautiful homes for photography.

Thanks also to the brave Sue McGovern for not running away screaming when I asked if she would help me to model the knits in this collection, as well as to Honor for being so patient.

Our trusty sample knitter Kim Hobley has helped to bring many ideas to life, thank you!

The knitalongs in our Ravelry group are lively, friendly and inclusive, and all gratitude is due to Alix, Katherine, Maylin and Nancy for their generous investment of time in supporting us with our group.

Jeni Hewlett and Andy Robinson have been kind and patient with everything from advice and encouragement, to yarn orders. Thank you both.

Finally, this book would not have happened without the encouragement of Kate Davies. We are incredibly thankful for the push to do it, and for the myriad advice on everything from accounting software to integrated shipping labels. Thank you.